TOWARDS INTEREST-FREE BANKING

Shaikh Mahmud Ahmad

KITAB BHAVAN
New Delhi-110002 (India)

KITAB BHAVAN
Publishers, Distributors, Exporters & Importers
1784, Kalan Mahal, Darya Ganj,
New Delhi - 1100 02 (India)
Phones : (91-11) 23277392 / 93, 23274686, 32906
Fax : (91-11) 23263383
Website : www.kitabbhavan.com
Email : nasri@vsnl.com
: nusrat@bol.net.in

Revised Edition ... 2000
IInd Edition ... 2009

ISBN : 81-7151-312-3
Book Code No. : T00032

Laser Typesetting at:
Laser Track
1784, Kalan Mahal, Darya Ganj,
New Delhi - 1100 02 [India]

Printed & Published in India by :
Nusrat Ali Nasri for KITAB BHAVAN
1784, Kalan Mahal, Darya Ganj,
New Delhi - 1100 02 [India]

Baya ke quaida-e-a'sman begardanaim
Qaza be gardashe ratl-e-giran begardanaim

(Ghalib)

Come forth, O spirits brave,
The heaven's mode we'll change,
Against our doleful fate
Our goblets large we'll range.

To

Tahir, Talat & Tayyab

with

all my love

Contents

INTRODUCTION

Though I have wrestled with various issues relating to Islamic economics for an entire life-time, for the last quarter century, I shifted over to an in-depth study of interest in the scientific context. Notwithstanding the complexity of the issue, from a humanistic point of view certain aspects attract attention to it, like the depredation that is an inescapable part of it, the perversions it inflicts on the functioning of every economy and deprivations that man has to suffer as its consequence. This naturally involves evaluation of the vast literature that has been produced in favour of this institution, because if interest is as equitable, fair and just as is made out by the bulk of capitalistic economics, it cannot lead to the sorry plight which the entire so called free world in general, and the Third World in particular, finds itself in.

The entire problem is obviously a scientific and technical one which can be properly handled only in a secular context. This approach becomes more compelling when we come to brass tacks, particularly the problem of how to evolve an interest-free banking structure. Since on this issue the pundits of economics and banking are sure that it cannot be done, one has to speak in their language if one happens to differ.

The result of all this effort has taken the form of a two volume study, entitled *Man and Money,* which is in the final stage of revision before publication. But even this process will not take less than a year, and naturally publication of a book more than ten times the size of the present one must take yet another year. In the mean time friends, who have read the larger manuscript in its entirety or in parts and regard it somewhat highly, have started feeling frustrated by what they call its "unending revisions." They therefore insisted that I leave aside the main work for a while and write a short book which brings out the salient points of the study within the context of the ideology of Islam and the vision of the founding fathers of this country. The result is the present book.

Yet, this is by no means a summary of *Man and Money*. There is not only the difference of context already mentioned above, but also of the fact that the larger work is far more concerned with the theoretical necessity of abolition of interest, and the repudiation of myths that have been evolved in its support, and the smaller one primarily focusses on the practical problem of evolving an interest-free banking structure. In fact, from this point of view, it goes farther than the larger work, as *Man and Money* does not concern itself with modalities and strategies of shift-over from an interest-oriented economy to an interest-free one, which is the subject of Chapter III of this book.

The main justification for publishing this book is that those interested in the subject, like the academician, the politician, the social thinker and, above all, the policy-maker, are likely to be too busy to give time and concentrated attention in the measure that the larger book will demand. So, the whole thing has been reduced to a capsule form, besides the effort to make it as readable as possible, with emphasis on the practical side of things.

Those who are not interested in the theoretical aspect of the issue, or are too busy to read the entire book, may skip over Chapter I. They can come back to it if they feel like it. On the other hand, those who find the theoretical enunciation a little too brief may wait for the publication of *Man and Money*.

Any academic body, political party, social forum, business federation, banking organisation, and planning or policy-making body that has questions to ask or clarifications to seek will find me willing to give my time for verbal elaboration according to mutual convenience. To make such an exercise meaningful, the proper course will perhaps be to formulate questions and indicate the nature of clarifications in advance to enable me to give due attention to them.

I am even more eager to learn and shall be grateful to any reader if he finds and communicates to me any factual or interpretative error. I shall be no less obliged if any other shortcomings of my approach or presentation are pointed out to me.

If any reader finds anything of value in this book, the credit should go to several friends including Mr. Mohammad Akram Khan, Mr. Enayatullah and Mr. Siraj Muneer without whose insistence, I could not have spared time to write it. I should also express my gratitude to Mr. Mohammad Akram Khan for his consistent help in providing creative criticism, understanding and enthusiastic support.

Mahmud Ahmad

CHAPTER – I
The Background

The Perspective in Brief

The struggle of man to liberate himself from the depredation of interest is as old as history itself, and predates even the minting of money.[1] Hammurabi, who ruled Babylonia from 2123 to 2081 B.C., has left us the oldest book in the world in the shape of his *Code*, which not only prescribes maximum rates of interest for various varieties of loans but also suggests the method of profit and loss sharing to avoid interest.[2] This is besides occasions on which no interest can be claimed.[3]

All great religions have opposed interest; from philosophers like Aristotle to poets like Dante, we repeatedly meet with repulsion for this institution. As Keynes puts it: "For several millenniums, enlightened opinion held for certain and obvious... the doctrine that the rate of interest is not self-adjusting at a level best suited to the social advantage..."[4] After discussing various theoretical problems revolving round the issue of its ineradicable consequences and its suppression he reached the conclusion that extinction of unemployment is not possible without "euthanasia of the rentier".[5]

The Difficulty of Elimination of Interest

The difficulty is that we do not know how to achieve "euthanasia of the rentier". Even Keynes concedes that "the average rate of interest which will allow a reasonable average level of employment is one so unacceptable to wealth-owners that it cannot be readily established."[6]

Forcible suppression of interest rate never proved workable. The main lesson we get from the experience of usury laws in Europe during medieval times is that forcible quashing or even reducing interest generates a black market for money loans at exorbitant interest rates.

This option being out, we are only left with devising a substitute for interest shorn of its exploitative content. Many ideas are available beginning with the idea of profit and loss sharing of Hammurabi's *Code*. The Jews, the Christians and the Muslims in turn adopted this idea, but each one of them found that it is limited in its workability. Any idea which does not encompass every variety of loan that can be demanded, cannot be regarded a suitable basis of banking. No idea has yet emerged which is free from this shortcoming.

Contribution of Jews

The first interest-free bank, by the name of Agibi Bank, was started by the Jews in Babylonia in 700 B.C.[7] The basis adopted was mortgage of some productive asset like a house, a piece of land, a horse or a slave etc., which the borrower parted with and the bank hired out in exchange of a loan without interest. Although an improvement on profit and loss-sharing concept it remains limited in its applicability as the deprivation of a productive asset imposes its own limitation. This again cannot be deemed capable of meeting all situations. For example, like profit and loss sharing, it has no answer to the problem of equating hire-purchase and cash purchase prices nor to that of encashment of bills of exchange without deduction of discount. The Jews met the intractability of the problem of encashment of bills of exchange by declaring discount to fall outside the ambit of interest, on the authority of Maimonides, one of their distinguished rabbis.[8] This means that even the financial wizardry of the Jews could find no adequate answer to the problem of elimination of interest.

Contribution of Christians

Under the patronage of Christian Church, the concept of service charge as substitute for interest was evolved. At first free loans were given following the precedent of Babylonian and Greek temples. Soon, it was found that small charges to cover working expenses were necessary. *Montes Pietatis,* as the lending institutions running on service charges were called, before long became indistinguishable from savings banks, paying a small interest on deposits and charging a higher rate on advances.[9] This exemplifies the unreliability of this concept as a workable substitute for interest. The concepts of triple contract and perpetual annuities, the only other significant concepts evolved under Christian influence are indistinguishable from interest.

Contribution of Muslims

No significant device has been evolved by Muslims as a substitute for interest. Their reliance on *shirkah* is no different from that of Hammurabi on profit and loss sharing and *mudarabah* is likewise a pre-Islamic arrangement.[10] Both suffer from identical inapplicability on a major part of economy. All effort has been to evolve some method of rewarding capital, and limitless subterfuges have been devised, from *Bai' al-'inah* to *Bai 'al-mu'ajjal* all as indistinguishable from interest as "mark-up", used as basis of banking in Pakistan.[11] No wonder the weekly *Economist* of London was forced to call it an "Islamic Fudge".[12] Post-revolutionary Iran, like some other lands claiming to have introduced Islamic banking, is playing a similar game of make-belief.

A small-scale pioneering experiment on the basis of profit and loss sharing was carried out in the shape of Mit Ghamr Saving Bank in Egypt, under the leadership of Dr. El Naggar, to attract small savings and support petty investments of productive character, on profit-sharing basis. Its limited applicability necessitated subsidy for its working, and when it ceased, the bank had to close.

Any number of investment banks run in various Muslim countries, making advances to solvent enterprises on the basis of *mudarabah* or *shirkah,* but not one of them will encash a commercial paper on face value, if it is short of maturity.

The sad reality is that though every one concedes that Islam prohibits interest, there is not a single Muslim country which is running its financial institutions without resorting to interest. The fact is that no one knows how to do it, and when political pressure mounts, they can only resort to some kind of subterfuge. Yet it is not necessary, perhaps not likely, that Islamic prohibition may end up in the way it did in the case of some earlier religions, because not only political pressure remains unabated, but indicates probability of further intensification.

The only concept available in Islamic thought which does not suffer from either a speck or a stain of interest is that of *qard hasan*. Though many pious Muslims have practised it in all times, no intellectual effort has been made to evolve an institutional framework on this basis.

Approach of Economists

Among humanists and economists, deeply conscious of the exploitative role of loan capital, we have the labour note scheme associated with the names of Owen, Bray and Rodbertus.[13] With some difference in details, we have the exchange bank theory of Proudhon.[14] The problem with Proudhon's circulating note, and labour note schemes mentioned earlier is exactly the one we have met in the case of encashment of commercial paper: how to equate deferred value with exactly equal present value. If we do it by discounting deferred value to strike equilibrium with present value, it means that we have yet to discover an alternative to interest. It is no surprise that Proudhon's bank did not work and had to be liquidated. This only shows that a clear perception of the level of Proudhon regarding the exploitative role of interest, including the manner in which it must generate unemployment, is not enough to devise an interest-free bank.

Keynes wanted us to extinguish interest if we desired to eliminate unemployment, but even he gave no guidance as to how to go about it. Keynesian economists left aside the ideal of Keynes, and tried to reach the same objective by pursuing expansionary fiscal and monetary policies. Keynes had suggested recourse to expansionism, *only after* interest had been reduced to what he called its "technical minimum" and which he estimated at around two per cent. But the pre-condition was forgotten, and unbridled expansionism was resorted to in the name of Keynes, and when it landed us in stagflation, *i.e.*, a combination of both stagnation and inflation, it started being said that even Keynesian advice had not worked. No one raised his little finger to suggest some way of reaching "euthanasia of the rentier", or at least the technical minimum suggested by Keynes.

The only exception is Switzerland and the results support the contention of Keynes. This country kept its bank rate close to technical minimum of Keynes. During a period of 35 years, from 1949 to 1983, bank rate has averaged 2.63 per cent.[15] Leaving U.A.E. and Kuwait out as special cases, Switzerland has the highest per capita income in the world.[16] Another even more remarkable achievement is virtual extinction of unemployment. During the decade of the 70's it has averaged 0.4 per cent.[17] In spite of these exceptional distinctions, its rate of inflation is the lowest in the world,[18] giving a lie to the contention of capitalistic economics that if unemployment is abolished, inflation must set in.

Germany and Japan lost the Second World War and U.K. and U.S.A. won it. But looking at the relative economic picture of these countries, it appears as though the victors were the vanquished and the vanquished, the victors. All kinds of explanations are given except the basic one, that the bank rate of the vanquished during their period of greatest growth has been, as a general rule, significantly lower than the bank rate of the victors. By way of partial illustration we find that according to I.M.F. figures *(Internation Financial Statistics Yearbook* for 1984) average annual bank rate during the decade of the 1970's in these four countries was 4.8% in West Germany, 6.12% in Japan, 9.45% in U.S.A. and 11.45% in U.K.

Contribution of Post-Keynesian Economists

With few exceptions, whoever among the Keynesian economists concerned himself with the issue of containment of interest did so in the context of expansionist philosophy of Beveridge. It was his *Full Employment in a Free Society,* first published in 1944, which veered economic thought and public policy alike from "euthanasia of the rentier" to expansionism as the answer to the problem of unemployment. It was the economics of Beveridge which assumed the name of Keynesian economics and became eminently entitled to be called, in the apt construction of Joan Robinson, "bastard Keynesianism",[19] even though used in a different context.

However, even expansionism calls for financial resources. These have to be secured on the basis of interest, even when resort is had to the printing press, involving perpetually increasing burden on the budget. Unlike Keynes, Keynesian economics concerned itself not with interest as such, but with reducing its burden on the exchequer. Harrod opines that loans contracted to fight unemployment should carry no interest, and suggests the creation of an independent Authority, governing Stabilization Fund which will generate the necessary interest-free resources.[20] It boils down to expansion of money supply through central bank without paying any interest to it.

In an identical proposal of Meade the name of the agency has changed to "Unemployment Assistance Board" which will finance itself by new notes issued by the Bank of England, on which no interest would be claimed.[21]

Similar is the approach of Wernette who visualizes a Federal Stabilization Board possessing "the power of creating new money, to be turned over to the federal government to finance budget deficits ... so as to ... maintain full employment".[22] These advances will presumably bear no interest.

Lerner throws overboard the intermediation of any agency and suggests resorting to "functional finance", meaning thereby to spend as much as eradication of unemployment calls for. He points out that if his prescription conflicts with "the principles of 'sound finance' or of balancing the budget or of limiting the national debt, so much the worse for these principles".[23]

Kurihara simplifies the whole thing by pointing out that government securities can be sold to the central bank, and even if interest is paid on these loans, eventually "part or all of it" will "go to the government".[24] Obviously, when central bank is nationalized, as is the case in Pakistan and many other countries, interest paid by the government to the bank comes back as revenue earned by the government on account of the running of the bank.

This is about the pinnacle which "bastard Keynesianism" could attain. Interest will stay, unemployment will stay, deficit budgets will be relied upon to reduce unemployment, the resource gap will be filled by printing of notes, whose practical shape will be that of borrowing from the central bank against government securities. When these banks are owned by governments, paying of interest will not matter, as this will amount to paying out of one pocket and receiving it back in the other.

Some like Wernette held that this policy will not generate any inflation.[25] Others like Vickrey saw in the inflationary possibilites of expansionism a built-in answer to the problem of reducing interest. According to him, interest at ten per cent, under a nine per cent inflationary arrangement, would mean reduction of real interest to one per cent.[26]

Governments around the globe have persistently pursued this policy and the results are before us all. Banishment of unemployment, which was the rationale for the adoption of this policy, is two to three times of what it was when this policy was adopted, apart from its being superimposed by inflation which has reduced the value of money to a fraction of what it was at that time. Stagflation has made it impossible to see any release from our predicament.

Perhaps it is time for us to return to the option of extinction of interest leading to elimination of unemployment, suggested by Keynes. So far as how to do it is concerned, we really do not have any significant idea, in the skeleton survey of man's struggle against interest, which can perform the function of running a credit system, without involving exploitation of the mass of people.

Obstacle in Earlier Ages

It is easy to reach the result that if human effort of 4000 years has not evolved an all-embracing unexploitative alternative to interest, it may perhaps be unattainable. That man can reach the moon, but cannot discover an unexploitative basis of advancing money loans appears, *prima facie,* a facile conclusion.

The fact is that during the ancient and medieval times, when exceptional intellectual effort was devoted to this issue, banking had not developed the level of sophistication it has attained in this age. The concepts developed during the past ages, like profit and loss sharing, mortgage and leasing, were far less inadequate during those times than these are at present.

The efforts of the people who keep trying to devise a model of modern banking by manipulating one or the other of these concepts is comparable to looking around to engage a dozen or more pairs of bullocks to pull a railway train, without realizing that we want the train to run at a speed which only an electric locomotive engine can give to it. Islamic economics, by and large, has not yet striven to go ahead of this level. The Report of the Panel of Experts in Pakistan, concerned with devising an interest-free credit structure for this country, eminently illustrates the statement.[27]

The Problem of Bias

Banking, although a hoary institution, developed many of its modern forms under the shadow of the industrial revolution. In the face of all-round development which was taking place on account of the inter-dependence of banking, trade and industry, it would have looked like inserting a spanner in the wheel of progress, if illegitimacy of interest and the privations it was projecting at the lowest rungs of the social strata were adequately emphasized. Bias in favour of money interests became a part of the ethos of economics. Marx must be given credit for raising the problem of bias, and accusing that economic theories were biased in a way opportune to the wealth-owning classes. Myrdal remarks, "In this he was undoubtedly correct".[28]

It is not essential that the economist may be necessarily conscious of his bias, "for a characteristic of biases is", explained Myrdal, "that the researcher is not conscious of them and does not have them under his control".[29] This explains why in the words of Haberler, "the theory of interest has for a long time been a weak spot in the science of economics",[30] and also why in the words of Vera and Friedrich Lutz "the theory of interest is, at present, in a state of great confusion".[31]

At times, this bias is conscious but few have the moral courage of Samuelson to admit it. He writes: "For at least another hundred years, we must pretend to ourselves and to every one that fair is foul and foul is fair; for foul is useful and fair is not. Avarice and usury and precaution must be our gods for a little longer still".[32] He does not indicate how he will justify this conscious pretension in view of his observation just five pages later that "the first duty of any discipline is to tell the truth".[33] He concedes that "At the zero rate of interest ... we could ... reach ... a kind of 'golden age' ".[34] Why should an economist of his competence raise a wall of pretensions in the way of the advent of that "golden age" passes ones comprehension, except in terms of the bias about which Myrdal insists. "It is my conviction that progress in our scientific work must begin with the elimination of bias".[35]

Compulsion of Tradition

According to Myrdal, apart from bias which is the common limitation of all social sciences because views emerge from viewpoints, economist works under the further limitation of "the impact of tradition, represented by a vast background of literature".[36] While this leaves space for considerable innovation and even controversy within the system, the flavour of methodological conservatism regarding the framework of the system is jealously protected. Fundamentals of the system are rarely permitted to be questioned, and the institution of interest is one of those fundamentals. On the intellectual level, Myrdal points out, "no vested interests are stronger than those rooted in ingrained thoughtways and preconceptions".[37]

Professional Bias

To this may be added professional vested interest. Myrdal testifies the situation: "Economists who have jobs and incomes outside the universities now probably constitute the majority of our profession. This new institutional situation has strengthened the forces operating for methodological conservatism. What is ordinarily demanded is that they be 'safe', 'sane' economists, having or on the way to acquiring prestige, and usually not the adventurous ones fighting for recognition of new ideas".[38]

Personal Bias

Closely related to it there is personal bias. All significant economists, like all policy-makers are likely to have interest-earning assets. It takes a large measure of self-denial to accept an argument which threatens to slash a significant measure of one's income. Even though prosperity may eventually, on elimination of interest, spread wide enough to make up for this loss even at the personal level, most people tend to prefer a bird in hand to two in the bush. In Pakistan, we have good enough example of a retired (now deceased) Auditor General of Pakistan, who spent most of his post-retirement life in legitimizing interest he had earned on his Provident Fund savings by trying to prove that Islam does not prohibit interest, and wrote a book to establish that point of view.[39] Others do not need to write books; it is enough to rely on chicanery whenever an argument is advanced for abolition of interest. That is why it becomes necessary for men of goodwill to assume the direction of events in their own hands, by acquiring awareness of the implications of this issue and mustering sufficient political clout to drown the petty personal considerations of the economists and policy-makers.

Increasing Isolationism of Modern Economics

Yet another contributory factor is the increasing isolation and unconcern of the economist with the dismal deprivations around him and his distancing himself from the fundamental responsibility of his discipline to provide the necessary leadership to alleviate man's misery. Not that he does not write on subjects of social relevance. In fact, ever since the socialist revolution in Russia, he writes more on these than he ever did before. But the constraint of remaining within what the environment is likely to regard as "safe" and "sane" limits, keeps him back from wrestling with the fundamental issues. It is therefore not exactly fair to ascribe it to what Myrdal calls "the great shrinkage of ordinary economist's training, interests and knowledge".[40] But consistent narrowing of outlook partly because of specialization is superimposed on the impalpable and yet imperative insistence of the environment on conformity. Gone are the days when a moral philosopher could become an Adam Smith, a stock broker a Ricardo, a theologian a Malthus, an engineer a Pareto, a social thinker a Mill, a philosopher a Marx, and a mathematician with wide-ranging literary and artistic sensibilities and a rewarding awareness of the trend of the market a Keynes. Right at this time when the ever-widening area of the complexities that an economist confronts so obviously call for a broad inter-disciplinary approach, he proceeds unconcerned in the direction of his own ever-deepening grooves.

Apart from isolation inherent in specialization, economics appears to be developing an inner tendency of unconcern with either the pulse of time or the throb of the human heart. Its increasing recourse to mathematical presentations, an assiduously cultivated fad, is elevating it to an etherial level from which it may not retain any contact with this dirty earth. Keynes who knew mathematics no less than economics had warned against it. He wrote "Too large a proportion of ... mathematical economics are mere concoctions, as imprecise as the initial assumptions they rest on, which allow the author to lose sight of the complexities and interdependencies of the real world in a maze of pretentious and unhelpful symbols".[41]

Untenability of Theories of Interest

Mathematics can help when the basic issues have outgrown the stage of contention. In relation to the problem in hand, leaving out some notable exceptions, like Bohm Bawerk's *Capital and Interest*, significant parts of Keynes' *General Theory* and parts of Harrod, Hawtrey and Kurihara, questioning the validity of interest, bulk of the effort of economics has been to justify it, yet not a single argument advanced in favour of this institution has a leg to stand on. All theories of interest evolved till the time of Bohm Bawerk, including those resting on productivity, abstinence and demand and supply concepts, were unanswerably repudiated by him. Yet economics continues whipping these dead horses, without evolving any persuasive answer to his criticism. It is not therefore necessary to repeat his arguments. Those interested in the evaluation of these theories must go to Bohm Bawerk himself, abridgement of whose close reasoning cannot avoid being less than fair to him. Additionally, constraint of space declines to yield. Only two significant theories, based on time-preference and liqudity-preference concepts, one of which he himself espoused escaped his scathing pen, but are as devoid both of logic and objective relevance as the theories he overthrew. To their evaluation, and that of some prevalent concepts supporting the institution of interest, we must give some space before proceeding further.

Time-Preference Theory

The basic concept in time-preference theory in Bohm Bawerk's own words is, "Present goods are, as a rule, worth more than future goods of like kind and number".[42] It is possible to show from his own writing that the opposite of this proposition is as true, and perhaps truer, than the proposition itself.

He concedes the importance of future well-being longed and cherished by all of us. "As a matter of fact, the future has a great place in our economical provision; a greater, indeed, than people usually think..it is a truth seldom seen in all its bearings, that our economical conduct has exceedingly little reference to the present, but is, almost entirely taken up with the future".[43] Whenever people save to provide for their future needs, their action is indisputable proof of the fact that they set higher store and assign higher value to identical goods in the future than in the present.

These two opposite realities, preferring present goods over future goods, and future goods over present goods, are well enough known to Bohm Bawerk. The former valuation is adopted by people who earn barely enough for their living, who cannot afford to save for their future, and in their case the notion of present goods being of greater value than future goods is undoubtably correct. But the concept takes a somersault when we bring into consideration the other people, whose income is well above the demands made by their immediate needs, so that they save, which means they consider, to the extent of their saving, future goods to be of greater value than the present goods. Bohm Bawerk concedes that position. Writes he: "To this category belongs, among others, that very considerable number of people whose income is obtained, mostly or altogether by personal exertion, and will, presumably, fall away at a later period of life when they become unfit for work ... It would seem that, in such cases, a present shilling should be less valued than a future one".[44]

How is it that in spite of recognizing this obvious reality he reaches an extraordinarily false conclusion? This is no occasion to go into all the details, but perhaps one staggeringly incorrect appraisal had quite something to do with it. Writes Bohm Bawerk: "The case, then, between present and future goods stands thus. The only possible uses of future goods are, naturally, future, while present goods have the same possibility of future use, and have besides according to choice —either the present uses, or those future ones which may turn up in the time that intervenes between the present moment and the future point of time with which the comparison is being made."[45]

This presentation is so obviously incorrect that except for having been "confounded by the touch of the Evil One",[46] there is no explanation as to why a person possessed of the scintillating intellect of Bohm Bawerk could allow himself to fall to such a deranged expression. He has confused even the simple concepts of the present and the future in this sentence. The present is the name of a point of time, *this moment,* whereas the future denotes a period of time, from here to eternity. It is the future goods which give us choice of consumption at any time after this moment, and not the present goods as he appears to argue. The present goods, namely the goods which give us more utility in the present than in the future, are the ones we will consume in this moment, and therefore these will not survive for consumption at any future time. The two varieties of goods cannot be confused. All goods consumed are present goods; all goods saved are future goods. What has been consumed has ceased to exist; it is therefore not possible to use it in the future as Bohm Bawerk suggests. On the other hand future goods are available at any point of time between the act of saving and the act of consumption of that saving. This is the basic superiority of future goods, their availability in contrast with extinction of present goods.

This leads us to a conclusion which is the exact opposite of the one reached by Bohm Bawerk. Those who prefer present goods over future goods, and to the extent they do so, are the ones who do not save. They therefore do not enter the money market, and hence play no part in the projection of their preference and institutionalizing it in the form of interest. Those who come to the money market are the ones who save, and who, by the very act of saving, indicate preference of future goods over present ones. If there is a bank that puts a premium on their preference and pays them interest, they will accept it, but they came to deposit the money in the bank because they preferred its future utilization to present use. So the notion of time preference, as developed by Bohm Bawerk, is applicable only in the case of those who do not save, but for this very reason is irrelevant because their preference is not projected in the money market; on the other hand, those who save are the very ones whose time preference is the exact opposite of what Bohm Bawerk regards it to be. So, in the one case, his theory is correct but irrelevant, and in the other, it is relevant but reality turns out to be the exact reverse of his projection. Either way the train of his theory declines to run on the rails of any variety of logic.

Liquidity Preference Theory

The *General Theory* of Keynes is not a cohesive or integrated book in the matter of guidance as to what we should do in the sphere of interest. His broad approach is to identify the areas of its exploitative manifestations. He spells out fifteen reasons[47] why it should be abolished, the most important of which are that unemployment must persist as long as interest stays,[48] and that the remedy for inflation is also to lower the rate of interest.[49] Though this may perhaps be the most revolutionary contribution of Keynes, it so seriously threatens some of the fundamental postulates of economics, that post-Keynesian economics has preferred to completely neglect this main thread which runs through the *General Theory*, and reaches its most unequivocal expression in his last chapter significantly entitled "Concluding Notes on the Social Philosophy Towards Which the *General Theory* Might Lead", Section II pages 374-377.

A second posture which recurs in the book is one of doubt whether institutional and psychological factors will allow interest to fall to a level at which full employment can be attained. He therefore feels forced to regard a "technical minimum" of around two per cent as necessary.[50]

His third concern related to the issue of interest is the

shortage of capital resources. He ponders over the reason as to why the world is "so poor as it is in accumulated capital assets," and reaches the conclusion that it can be explained "neither by the improvident propensities of mankind, nor even by the destruction of war, but by the high liquidity premium ... attaching to money."[51] This is the mental background, the intellectual concern, which gives birth to the concept of liquidity preference. On account of this concept, we reach the stage where a low rate of interest, say two per cent, "leaves more to fear than to hope".[52]

What was the hope and what is the fear? The hope was that with every reduction of interest rate, the hazard of enterprise will fall and its profitability will rise, leading to expansion and deepening of all varieties of investment, with the consequence of going a long distance towards reducing unemployment, when interest falls to its "technical minimum" of two per cent.

Now what is the fear? The fear is that interest "being the reward for parting with liquidity",[53] at such a low rate of interest people may like to keep their savings uninvested. This being precisely the time for investment why should people like to keep their savings in a liquid form? He gives three considerations which may persuade them to stay liquid. He names them transactions motive, precautionary motive and speculative motive. Due to these considerations, the fear is that long before reducing interest to zero, even at two per cent interest "liquidity preference may become virtually absolute in the sense that almost every one *prefers cash to holding a debt which yields so low a rate of interest*"[54] (Italics added).

If it could be established that at low rate of interest, people will literally prefer "cash to holding a debt which yields so low a rate of interest", the theory will stand proved and the purpose of the theory fulfilled in explaining why the world is so short in capital resources. But that involves proving that people at two per cent interest will start keeping their savings inside their mattresses or their pillows or create hidden hollows in the wall or under the floor to stack them. However much Keynes may have erred in the formulation of this theory, he stopped short of relying on the absurd conclusion of his logic. He therefore resiles from this preposterous position by first replacing the word "money" in place of liquid savings, and including "time deposits with banks and, occasionally even such instruments as *(e.g.)* treasury bills"[55] in his definition of liquid savings.

Now this is no ordinary twist of logic. This amounts to pulling out the entire foundation of the theory, after which the superstructure of the theory has no place to go to except falling flat. Once liquid saving goes to a bank, however much it may remain liquid for the depositor, it becomes a part of the social money stream, from which the borrowers can borrow, within the limits prescribed by the statutory reserve. As soon as savings are out of mattresses and pillows and into time deposits and treasury bills, these cease to be a case in which people prefer "cash to holding a debt which yields so low a rate of interest."[56] They have already unequivocally indicated their preference for "holding a debt" to "holding cash" and in so doing repudiated the theory.

How then do we explain the scarcity of capital, which Keynes wanted to elucidate with the help of this theory? The real point of contraction of capital resources is not the liquidity of saving but the bank reserve, which has nothing to do with the three motives spelled out by Keynes. It is this bank reserve, and this alone, which is a self-contrived arrangement for scarcity of capital. It is not the logic of Keynes remarkably bearing the stamp in this case of having been "confounded by the touch of the Evil One"[57] but the bias of economics which forces it to accord acceptance to this theory.[58] It is the same bias which has compelled economics to give acceptance to every other theory of interest as well, although every one is as devoid of logic and of empirical support as liquidity preference theory happens to be.

Interest And Deposit Mobilization

Intellectual bankruptcy, which is the hallmark of every theory of interest, without a single exception, is also shared by every other concept hitherto propounded to support this exploitative institution. Let us take the deposit mobilization capability interest is credited with. The present writer gathered statistics relating to a ten year period, 1971-1980, of bank deposits and real rates of interest in five countries, *viz.*, Germany, Japan, Switzerland, U.K. and U.S.A. Out of these 50 period-countries, in 33 period-countries real interest rates were a minus category,sometime extending to double digit level, without indicating any impact on persistent increase in bank deposits in *even a single case.* So, if negative interest of even double digit dimension does not hurt deposit mobilization, zero rate of interest cannot possibley do so.[59]

Scarcity Being Self-Contrived Does Not Justify Interest

Similarly, devoid of reality is the apparently persuasive argument that since capital is a scarce commodity, and every scarce commodity has got to have a price, there is no reason for capital to be denied its price which is what is called interest. This argument in support of interest should win the case for it hands down, if it were not for the fact that scarcity is artificially manipulated through the institution of bank reserve. If we do not raise artificial barriers in the flow of credit, and devise a system of banking in which the outflow of advances keeps an absolute balance with the inflow of deposits, which, of course, is not possible without reducing banking reserve to zero, the scarcity of capital ceases to exist. The argument would not stand if it could be proved that an alternative banking structure, shorn of statutory reserve is impossible to invent. But reason cannot be stretched that far, because no one has yet looked into this aspect of the issue. Till this aspect is gone into, it is not possible to accept scarcity of capital, because of the contrivance which produces it, as a sufficient justification for the institution of interest. That is why Keynes declared "there are no intrinsic reasons for the scarcity of capital."[60] That being so, there is no intrinsic reason left for charging a price for this contrived scarcity.

Opportunity Cost of Capital an Obsolete Concept

Similarly, development of banking has made the opportunity cost of capital an obsolete concept. When a person saves an amount, he deposits it in a bank; when he needs it, he withdraws that amount, and yet receives interest for the period for which his deposit stayed in the bank, even if his deposit is a time-deposit and his withdrawal a pre-mature one. Opportunity cost of capital cannot explain interest earned in a prematurely withdrawn time deposit. On which day is an opportunity lost to the saver on account of depositing his saving in a prematurely withdrawable bank deposit, which stays for a period in the bank, during the pleasure and absolute option of the saver, and yet earns interest, is obviously an unanswerable question.

The context in which schoolmen found themselves forced to accord acceptance to this concept under the nomenclature of "extrinsic titles" is long since extinct. The Christian Church was impressed by the argument in the context of *individual* lending and borrowing. It is possible to argue that when one individual lends another an amount of money, the lender may have to forego availing himself of opportunities that come his way during the period of the loan. Another possible loss of opportunity can occur if the borrower fails to return his loan at the expiry of the period for which he borrowed it. This can result in considerable loss to the lender, as he may have to borrow on interest to meet his business commitments.

Neither of these two losses of opportunity or even the fear of their occurrence is experienced in the case of any interest earning bank deposit, say, a saving bank or a time deposit. One can withdraw one's deposit even prematurely and yet earn interest, although at the saving bank instead of the time deposit rate. The likelihood of any bank declining to pay out the deposited money at the expiry of the stipulated time is so close to zero as not to be worthy of consideration.

Opportunity cost of capital exists only so long as we consider the issue in the frame of individual lending and borrowing. The moment we shift evaluation of the concept to the context of institutionalized lending and borrowing, as we must in the interest of realism, the issue of opportunity cost of capital does not arise at all.

Rationing Capability of Interest is a Myth

The claim that interest performs a useful function in allocating scarce resources to most desirable creative activities is repudiated by objective reality. Today, much more than one-half of the loanable resources in the so-called free-world are utilized to cover the budgetary deficits of respective governments. Two examples will suffice. In Pakistan, between the years 1975 and 1982, the fiscal deficit of the government formed 64.98 per cent of total increase in deposits in the banks of Pakistan during these years. The figures for U.S.A. are even more remarkable. The budgetary deficit of U.S.A. for the period 1974-83 forms 107.17 per cent of total increase in deposits in American banks during this period.[61] If globally nearly three-fourths of allocable resources are gobbled up by a single item which is not only not productive, but conceivably the most counter-productive of all allocations, to credit interest with capability to "ration scarce resources" can be subscribed to only by scholars who give long leave to their critical faculties while reading mythologies spun out by economics.

Even leaving this glaring repudiation of the concept out of our consideration, we find that banks have no concern with the qualitative appraisal of the project for which a loan is sought, but only with the credit-worthiness of the party which seeks a loan. Even though it is self-obvious, it can also be empirically proved. If by way of example, we look at the construction industry in Pakistan, we find palatial houses, massive multi-storey flats, major shopping plazas being built on all sides in all our major cities; and not far from these construction sites, we find hutments and slums of the poor, extending over even vaster areas. The argument is that we are short of houses and short of business premises. Are we really that short of houses of rental value of four and five figures, and not at all of those of two or three figures, that our banking system is directing such a large chunk of credit to the costlier variety of houses? Interest is obviously unconcerned with any variety of allocation, except showering benefits on those who measure up to, its demand of credit-worthiness, irrespective of what they do with the loans they secure.

Wicksellian Confusion Regarding Interest and Prices

Never has a more illustrious economist evolved a more incorrect theory than the inverse relationship visualized by Wicksell to obtain between interest and prices. According to him a certain level of "average rate of interest" has got to exist so that "the general level of prices has no tendency to move either upwards or downwards". If the rate is fixed below this level, "no matter how small the gap, prices will rise and will go on rising..." If interest is raised above "the natural rate, prices will fall continuously and without limit".[62]

The conflict of his thesis with the reality of economic life was fully known to Wicksell. Tooke's monumental *History of Prices* which Wicksell had read, gave limitless evidence that falling commodity prices are associated in actual experience, not with a rising rate of interest but with a falling one. His intellectual probity and moral courage are both reflected when he concedes, "It had always been observed that .. a low discount rate accompanies low and not high prices, while an abnormally high discount rate is scarcely ever found to prevail except when commodity prices are high".[63]

Nevertheless, he himself went into the issue of empirical reality in the matter of relationship between interest and prices. He collected his own figures of both these magnitudes, covering a period of 45 years, from 1850 to 1895 of Berlin and London markets. He drew a curve to illustrate his findings which is available in his *Selected Papers on Economic*

Theory, page 87, which only confirms Tooke's findings. He does not hesitate to concede that "a high rate of interest is associated with high commodity prices and a low rate of interest is associated with low commodity prices, rather than the other way round."[64]

Yet this overwhelming inductive evidence against his theory does not deflect him from pressing it further. He explains his sticking to his theory by declaring "faithful to the principle we established earlier, however, we are not going to let ourselves be put out by this circumstance but, for the time being, we shall test the theory on the grounds of logic."[65]

When we closely examine his logic, we find that his short term illustration leads to a conclusion exactly opposite to the one he wants us to reach. Both of his long term examples are based on two assumptions, *viz.*, full employment and absence of technological advancement restricting the need for labour, which are so unrealistic that conclusions reached by him can only be regarded the result of confused thinking of a variety one cannot possibly expect from a scholar of his eminence.[66] Like Bohm Bawerk's time preference concept and Keynes liquidity preference theory, Wicksell's inverse relation argument between interest and prices can only be explained by the magic spell of "the touch of the Evil One".[67]

Above all any theory, however meticulously formulated, and however illustrious its authorship, if it does not reflect reality and disdains to keep its feet on this dirty earth, is not worth the paper on which it is written. Subsequent to Wicksell, many studies of relationship between interest and prices have been undertaken, and although all reach the conclusion of direct relationship between the two, repudiating his inverse relationship thesis, yet meticulously avoid affirming it except in suppppressed, defensive tones; so widespread is the impact of "the touch of the Evil One". Keynes sums up the empirical position by saying, "the broad character of the statistics since 1820 can be summarised as follows. Prices and interest fell together from 1820 to 1850, rose together from 1851 to 1856, fell together in 1857 to 1858, rose together from 1858 to 1864, fell together from 1866 to 1869, fell together from 1873 to 1896, rose together from 1896 to 1900, fell together from 1901 to 1903, rose together from 1905 to 1907, fell together in 1907 to 1908, rose together from 1908 to 1914 and 1914 to 1920, and fell together from 1920 to 1923. And over and above these general trends, a number of minor oscillations of the two are in the same direction".[68] Keynes concedes that direct relationship between interest and prices is "one of the most completely established empirical facts within the whole field of quantitative economics, though theoretical economists have mostly ignored it".[69] So far as the present writer is aware, this perversion remains the standard stock of text-book economics. Keynes alone struck the note of acceptance of reality in his *General Theory* when he affirmed that "Thus the remedy for the boom is not a higher rate of interest, but a lower rate of interest".[70]

Though Wicksellian thesis is not a theory of interest, it serves the purpose of providing a reason for interest to stay, ostensibly in order to protect the value of money. Notwithstanding its poverty of logic and compulsive empirical repudiation, its finding remains the stock of trade of both text-book economics and public policy. Its repudiation is therefore necessary for clearing the intellectual undergrowth before we can prepare ourselves to build a road to interest-free banking.

Inflation as Argument For Retention of Interest

Ever since the mid 1960's the entire so-called free world is living under a regime of persistent inflation, providing yet another reason for interest to stay. If no return is paid to the depositor, his savings over the years will continue suffering depletion in real value which can lead to a situation in which savings in aggravated circumstances may cease altogether.

The first answer to this argument is that retaining interest and even raising its level is no guarantee that inflation at a level higher than that of interest will not obtain, creating persistent nibbling of the value of saving, notwithstanding retention of interest. This is what is actually happening in most of the years in most of the countries. The present writer studied the situation in this regard during a ten year period, from 1971 to 1980, obtaining in five countries, *viz.*, Germany, Japan, Switzerland U.K. and U.S.A. The rate of inflation was often higher than the rate of interest with the result that the real rate of interest was a negative entity in U.K and Germany in 6 years out of 10, in Japan in 9 years out of 10, in Switzerland in 8 years out of 10 and in U.S.A. in 4 years out of 10. So, retention of interest has provided no guarantee against reduction in real value of savings. Of course one could go to the extent of indexation of saving, which would involve indexation of much else including prices, wages and profits ending up in a fascist arrangement of the entire economy.

But if we want to retain free institutions and also retain the value of savings we shall have to concentrate on the reason for emergence of inflation and whether there is any method by which it can be halted. The line of causation which ended up in persistent inflation is fairly clear. At the end of the 2nd World War, we were concerned with the prospect of depression and of widespread unemployment. There were two ways open to us. The Keynesian way prescribed "euthanasia of the rentier" which did not appear acceptable to us. We therefore opted for the Beveridgean way of expansionism, disregard of fiscal discipline, and wide ranging social security apparatus. To invest our choice with the authority of Keynes, we called it Keynesian economics, though Keynes had specifically cautioned against this interpretation of his doctrine.

When persistent fiscal deficit, feeding upon itself, crossed the limits of resilience of free world economies, as it did around mid 1960's, continuous inflation was the natural consequence. In one word, it is our refusal to eliminate interest which Keynes had advised us to adopt as the principle of our policy which has landed us in inflation. If we had adopted his advice, we neither needed consumptional expansionism, nor the vast social security apparatus, nor the crushing public debt, nor the fiscal irresponsibility from which we can now find no escape. Obviously, to overcome this inflation, and save the real value of savings is to go back to the point where we took the wrong road and start serious consideration of the methodology of elimination of interest which may ensure productive expansionism along with extinction of unemployment, excluding the necessity of fiscal indiscipline, which is responsible for inflation. In short, inflation is not a good enough argument for retention of interest, but a far more persuasive one for its elimination.

Confusion Between Concepts of Interest and Profit

Any layman can answer the question as to what is the difference between interest and profit. Economics is fully aware that these are two factor costs that have to be paid to two different varieties of contributions made, or supposed to be made, by capital and enterprise. Yet there has to be some unwritten law in the ethos of economics which dictates that the boundary between these two words should be so overlaid with some variety of impenetrable mist that the exact delimitation of the two should become impossible. The method generally adopted by most economists beginning with Adam Smith is to mix up the two fundamental terms by the use of word profit for interest with a fair degree of frequency, and on occasion, even the word interest for profit, so that the objective of confusion does not slip out of hands. It is not possible in this small book either to illustrate at any significant length the misuse of these words in the hands of several distinghished economists, nor to evaluate the compulsions which lead to it and the consequences that emerge from it.[71] To give just one illustration, one may look up Samuelson's *Economics*, one of the best text books on the subject, written by one of the most competent living economists. He uses the word profit almost as many times in the meaning of interest as for what the word actually means. In fact, he explicitly affirms that the two words are virtually interchangeable. If the reader does not believe it, he may read the following two brief extracts:

> "The lower is the interest rate (or profit rate – they are the same thing in absence of uncertainty) ..."[72] (Parenthesis Samuelson's own).
>
> "Even today, if the profit rate (pure interest rate plus premium to cover risk) were forced down..."[73] (Parenthesis Samuelson's own).

We shall confine ourselves to just three examples to illustrate the point that some economists, even when they are conscious of the undesirability of this confusion, tend to contribute to it. Bohm Bawerk states that "Lauderdale, like Adam Smith and Ricardo, does not distinguish between interest... and ... profit, but groups both under the name of profit."[74] Exactly three pages after this remark, Bohm Bawerk himself uses the phrase "net interest or profit."[75]

Cassel admits that "the distinction between interest and profit... is... of the greatest practical importance."[76] But exactly two pages before it he writes about the "ordinary usurer who draws his profit from the borrower."[77]

Conard notes that Schumpheter regards identification of interest and profit as a fundamental error,[78] yet he can question interest by calling it "net profit".[79]

It is true that this is not always done and some distinguished economists never commit this mistake,[80] yet the misuse is resorted to with sufficient frequency to squeeze out capability of capitalistic version of economics to identify the basic source of rampant exploitation, much less enable it to help us in devising an alternative to interest, shorn of its depredation.

Socialistic Economics Accentuates This Confusion

Though socialistic economics developed as a reaction to its capitalistic version, it only perpetuates the confusion between interest and profit, in spite of the inverse approach dictated by their respective positions. The capitalistic version appears motivated to extend to interest, against which there is a hoary history extending to serveral millenniums, the acceptability which has generally been available to profit as a reward for enterprise. The mixing up of the two terms seems to have been persisted in to serve the interest of the capitalist as distinguished from the enterpreneur, by accentuating the confused area between the two.

Socialistic economics instead of tearing away this curtain of make-belief preferred to take the capitalistic version at its word. If interest and profit are the same thing, and interest is obviously exploitative, profit should be regarded no less so. In socialistic economics the word profit is almost always used to include interest and even rent, and capitalist means both what it should as well as the entrepreneur.

Marx knew the difference between these two factor costs. He regards "money exchanged for more money, a form that is incompatible with the nature of money... therefore the usurer is most rightly hated..."[81] He quotes with approval Martin Luther, who gave as good a definition of interest as can be: "Whoever takes more or better than he gives, that is usury, and is not service".[82] He knows the contribution made by the entrepreneur. "With the keen eye of an expert", he writes, "he has selected the means of production and the kind of labour best adapted to his particular trade..."[83] Again, the entrepreneur, called the "capitalist" as usual, takes "good care that the work is done in a proper manner, and that the means of production are used with intelligence, so that there is no unnecessary waste of raw material..."[84]

He had all the clarity of perception to build on these foundations the superstructure of his theory. Yet he does not avail himself of the opportunity, and evolves a concept of surplus value which includes besides interest and rent, remuneration to the labour of management.

The fact is that all socialist writers from Sismondi to Samir Amin are even more confused regarding the difference between interest and profit than even capitalistic economists happen to be. The consequence is that, leaving aside exceptions like Keynes, Harrod, Hawtrey and Kurihara, we do not have any clear enunciation of the unadulterated nature of exploitation projected by interest or the creative nature of labour which is rewarded with profit, in the two main versions of available economics. Since necessity for elimination of interest cannot even be felt before this cardinal difference between these two factor costs can be realized, to expect either of these two versions of economics to help us in evolving a methodology for elimination of interest, is to ask for something on which they have hitherto felt no need to apply their expertise.

Enter Islamic Ideology

The emergence of Islamic ideology is a part of the resurgence of Islam in many Muslim countries in general, and of the creation of Pakistan in particular. The *raison d'etre* for the creation of this country was that the Muslims of the sub-continent wanted to design their polity in a way which enabled them to live their corporate life in consonance with the ideology of Islam.

The motivating factor was the belief that in this new country, by following the provisions of Islamic economy, we will be able to eradicate poverty. Iqbal, one of the greatest poets of this century and one of the greatest seers of all time, whose vision is responsible for the emergence of this country, hinted as early as his famous Allahabad address of 1930, that Islam had a creative "social structure regulated by a legal system".[85] According to him "nature of the Holy Prophet's religious experience... is... creative of a social order."[86] In his rebuttal of articles by Pandit Jawaher Lal Nehru, in the late 1930's, he singles out the potential capability of the traditions and heritage of Islam to provide livelihood to all which cannot be achieved in a united Indian culture.

In his letters to Jinnah, persuading him to demand a separate country for the Muslims of the sub-continent, Iqbal first poses the question, "how is it possible to solve the problem of Muslim poverty"[87] He proceeds to answer, "Happily there is a solution in the enforcement of the Law of Islam and its further development in the light of modern ideas. After a long and careful study of Islamic Law, I have come to the conclusion that if this system of law is properly understood and applied, at least the right to subsistence is secured to everybody. But the enforcement and development of the *shariat* of Islam is impossible in this country without a free Muslim state or states".[88] He calls Islam a "social democracy" and claims "For Islam, the acceptance of social democracy in some suitable form is not a revolution, but a return to the original purity of Islam".[89]

Quaid-e-Azam Muhammad Ali Jinnah concedes in his Foreword to these letters that Iqbal's "views were substantially in consonance with my own and had finally led me to the same conclusions".[90]

So, the primary purpose of the creation of this country was to solve the problem of poverty through a recourse to the evolution of Islamic heritage in the economic sphere in the context of today. By implication, this indicated disenchantment with both the prevalent economic systems. Iqbal explicitly repudiates both in his poetry repeatedly. About capitalism, his view is that it has already reached the end of its tether:

> *"Giya daur-e-sarmaya daree giya"*
>
> (The age of capitalism has come to its end)

About socialism, he visualizes Satan addressing his advisers:

> *"Mazdakiyyat fitnae farda naheen Islam hai"*
>
> (The real problem of tomorrow is Islam and not socialism)

He closes his masterpiece of poetic work, *Javid Nama,* with a poem, whose opening verse is:

> *"Beguzar az khawaro afsoonye afrang masho.*
> *Ke nayarzad be jaway een hama daireena-o-nao"*

The verse has been translated as under:

Be not enchanted by the West
Nor on the East thou needest dote
For both this ancient and this new
Together are not worth an oat.[91]

He is specific in the matter of interest. Significantly, it is in the message of Jamal-ud-Din Afghani to the Russians that the following verse occurs:

*"Az riba akhar cheh mee zaid? fitan
Kas nadanad lazzati qarz-i-hasan"*

What usury breeds save tension all around?
Of the bliss of noble lending none's aware.

He visualizes the emergence of a new civilization whose foundational principles he spells out in *Javid Nama*. His first principle is *Khilafat-e-Adam, i.e.* viceregency of Man. Naturally dignity of man has got to be the core of that principle. He himself explicitly underscores it:

*"Bartar az gardoon maqame adam ast
Asle tahzeeb ihtarame Adam ast"*
Man's lofty rank is higher far than heave'n
On his respect is civilization based.

So, the foundational principles which Iqbal evolves for the emergence of Islamic civilization, in the economic sphere, were to devise an economy in which bread should be available to all, without depriving any one of his dignity. One of the main instruments through which he visualized the attainment of this objective was the evolution of an interest-free economy.

Enter Islamic Economics

Islamic economics had exactly identical objectives and instruments for its guidance spelled out not only by Iqbal but the Quran itself. The Holy Book gives expression to its objective in the economic sphere by employing the remarkable construction of *rizkun kareem* (24:26 and four other places). Allama Yusuf Ali translates these words as "provision honourable"; in prosaic language we could call it "bread with dignity", with a connotation of adequacy.

The Quran spells out three major instruments for the attainment of this objective. The first one is the instrument of free enterprise *ahallallahul bai'a* (2:275), the second is eradication of exploitation through elimination of interest *wa harrama al-riba* (2:275), and the third is a cardinal concern with egalitarian purpose and social justice raised to the level of a pillar of the faith under the title of *zakat*.

This sharply distinguishes the difference of Islamic economics from the capitalistic and socialistic versions of this discipline. Capitalism accepts both profit and interest; socialism, at least in theory, rejects them both, while Islam accepts profit motive and rejects interest.

Another advantage with which Islamic economics could make its start was that the definition of interest is provided by the Quran itself. If *lakum ru'us amwalikum* (2:279) is read with *zaroo ma baqiya min al-riba* (2:278) we easily reach the definition of *riba*.Any excess above the borrowed sum is interest. So from the Islamic point of view, the only permissible rate of interest is zero. Unless Islamic economics first defines interest, and that definition is in conformity with the one given by the Quran, it cannot possibly devise an interest-free credit structure. This excludes the possibility not only of our being able to arrange a cease-fire with Allah and His Prophet, for the Quran regards insistence on interest as "declaration of war against Allah and His Prophet" (2:279), but also lose out of hand the glorious possibility of evolving a new civilization capable of providing an in-built assurance of "provision honourable" for which the spirit of man has yearned from the dawn of history.

Unfortunately, Islamic economics has yet to reach even its starting point. Without looking into the possibility whether some mechanism can be devised by which lending and borrowing on zero rate of interest may be possible, feasible and workable, it appears overweighed by the considerations that capitalistic economics advances for the retention of this institution, notwithstanding the fact that, as we have already seen above, these are hollow to the core. This hesitation is apparently buttressed by the feeling that since no alternative to interest has yet been evolved, it must therefore be impossible to devise. No one has cared to study the rigorous efforts made by the rabbis and schoolmen, under the influence of Judaism and Christianity respectively, the obstacles they confronted, and whether these can be removed in the context of the new banking modalities that have emerged. No one appears to have pondered over the tantalizing possibility of raising an edifice of banking on the concept of *qard hasan*. No revolutionary achievement in history has been made without the will to do a thing, mustering necessary courage to tread uncharted paths, and cheerfully face the rigours involved in every such option. Not that there is any dearth of these essential ingredients, but they are all devoted to discovering a subterfuge for interest, instead of devising a banking structure which may have the in-built capability of excluding its necessity altogether. Our efforts at substitution boil down, however unconscious of it we may be, to perpetuation of interest under one garb or another. More than any other Islamic economist, the present writer is guilty of this dereliction. His *Economics of Islam*[92] was perhaps the first to argue that the concept of *shirkah* is capable of being developed as a basis of interest-free banking in the modern context. This was a stupendous error. Though much better books on Islamic economics have since been written, the error has not yet been squeezed out.

What Is Wrong With *Shirkah*?

Shirkah and *Mudarabah* are excellent devices to eliminate interest in personal dealings, though even at that level they have no answer to issues like encashment of commercial paper and hire-purchase of anything. As soon as we enter the realm of institutional credit, the workability of both these concepts contracts, while problems connected with their application multiply, rendering both these concepts virtually obsolete.

The first significant pointer towards their obsolescence is that in most so-called free countries the bulk of loanable resources are required by governments to cover their fiscal deficit. Taking the example of Pakistan, the consolidated over-all deficit of Federal and Provincial Governments for the financial year 1986-87 was 53.64 billion rupees.[93] The total increase in demand and time deposits from July 1986 to June 1987 was only 25.48 billion.[94] True, this was a particularly bad year from budgetary deficit point of view for Pakistan, but banking structure has to cater for all kinds of eventualities. Neither *shirkah* nor *mudarabah* has any answer to this situation.

By definition, these have no answer to any variety of consumptional loans. Even in the case of productive loans, the number of borrowers precludes supervisory arrangements under either of these two concepts. At the end of March 1987, their number in Pakistan was above 1.5 millions.[95] No supervisory mechanism can oversee actual results obtained in the functioning of such a large number of borrowers. The only workable method, if we insist on sticking to these obsolete concepts, will be drastically curtailing the number of borrowers, and excluding every one except a very selective portion of corporate borrowers. If we take this relatively viable route, it will drastically increase unemployment with possible explosive political consequences.

It is obvious that no viable structure of banking can be raised on the basis either of *shirkah* or *mudarabah*.

Bai‘ al-Mu’ajjal

Some *fuqaha*, though not all, have accepted validity of *bai‘ al-mu’ajjal*, sanctioning difference between spot and future prices of any commodity. This naturally opens the way for encashment of bills of exchange after deduction of discount, and facilitates hire-purchase in the same way as interest does. It is not realized that if we accept the difference between spot and future prices of commodities, we cannot logically reject interest which is also an identical difference between the spot and future prices of a commodity called by the name of money. In view of this fact, we do not need to argue why it is a mere stratagem to avoid the name of interest and yet retain its substance.

We have direct prohibition of the Holy Prophet to indulge in this variety of *bai'*. He has forbidden two sales in a single sale. *Naha 'an bai'ataini fil bai'ah.*[96] Besides *Muwatta,* this *hadith* is reported in *Tirmidhi, Ahmad* and *Nasa'i.* Allama Waheed-uz-Zaman, commentator of *Muwatta* has given the meaning of this *hadith* as prohibition from buying a commodity which has different spot and future prices.[97] The Holy Prophet is even more explicit elsewhere: *Man bai'aa bai'ataini falahu aukasuhuma awar-riba.*[98] "Anything which has two prices (spot and future) must be purchased at the lower price, otherwise it will become usury."

Mark-up

Mark-up adopted in Pakistan as a substitute for interest, is really a mix-up of the prohibited *bai' al-mu'ajjal* with equally disapproved *bai' al-'inah.* The device adopted is that a fictitious deal is entered into between the borrower and the bank, in which the bank purchases certain goods from the borrower, thus lending money to him. The bank entitles itself to claim back its loan along with interest (called mark-up) by stipulating simultaneously in the same agreement that the borrower will purchase back the same goods from the bank at the expiry of a certain period during which the price of goods will be marked up at the rate of 47 (or more) paisas per thousand rupees per day.

The logic behind this arrangement is that a bank has every right to purchase a commodity, and also every right to sell it on profit, even to the same party from which it was purchased.

There are three objections to this arrangement. The first is the fixity of the mark-up at some specific level, generally 47 paisa per thousand rupees per day, which works out to 17.15% interest per year. We have only changed the name of interest to mark-up (and in the process raised the rate of interest from 14% to 17.15%) and claim we have abolished interest.

The second objection is that this variety of purchase and sale is prohibited by the Holy Prophet. He has emphatically declared: *La bai'a ma laisa 'indak.*[99] You cannot sell a thing which you do not possess. Neither the borrower has the commodity which he sells to the bank at the time of borrowing, nor the bank has the commodity which it resells to the borrower at the time of the return of the loan along with "mark-up".

Thirdly, common sense would never permit this arrangement. Where is the sale and where is the resale? The bank and the borrower only enter into an agreement in writing that so and so sells such and such a thing to this particular bank for this amount and will buy back the same thing from the bank at the end of such and such a period during which he will pay mark-up at such and such a rate. No commodity of any kind passes hands either way. It is all notional, all make-belief, all myth, all pretension.

And we claim, we have abolished interest!

It is not clear whom we are cheating. Allah and His Prophet cannot be cheated, however clever our manipulation may be, and this one is not even that. In the language of Quran we remain at war with Allah and His Prophet for persisting in interest (2:279). Some people may be cheated for a while, but even they will not be for all time. We are cheating the aspirations of the masses. We are cheating the dreams of a million martyrs who gave their lives to create this country. We are cheating the core and substance of the vision of Iqbal. We are cheating the destiny of this country. We are snatching the glory of our future with our own two hands. We are throwing out of our hands the possibility of the emergence of the Third Way which can simultaneously guarantee both bread and dignity to man. We are cheating out the emergence of a new civilization.

Current Posture of Islamic Economics

The worst part of the story is that Islamic economists as a body in their International Monetary and Fiscal Conference held in Islamabad in 1981, gave their unreserved approval to this arrangement. So far this is the best that Islamic economics has to offer, *viz.*, change the name of interest and you have abolished interest.

In private conversation many Islamic economists would be willing to admit that this is no solution at all but few have thought it prudent to openly express themselves. Professional and academic bias, we saw in the context of capitalistic economics, is at work with redoubled impact in the sphere of Islamic economics. In the words of Myrdal, every one wants to be considered a "safe" and "sane" economist. We do not have a single Samuelson who may have the moral courage to admit that in retaining interest we are playing a game of pretension necessitated by such and such reason.

The Basic Obstacle

The second and even more overwhelmingly basic obstacle is that interest is sought to be abolished generally within the matrix of capitalistic economics, or on occasion in that of socialistic economics, both of which present insuperable hurdles. There is no such thing as Islamic capitalism or Islamic socialism because these are bound to boil down, for all practical purposes, to capitalism and socialism respectively. Abolition of interest alone involves rewriting of entire economics from end to end, and obviously Islamic economics is a lot more than abolition of interest. Mere scholarship which is often there, even when accompanied by insight and vision, which are sometime in evidence, are not enough. This kind of work also demands courage of conviction, exceptional critical competence and willingness to undertake nerve-racking, back-breaking hard work, which do not appear to be in adequate supply.

The nature of the difficulty will perhaps become clearer by giving a specific example. If one is intellectually persuaded to subscribe to one or the other theory of interest, or concurs in the concept of capital scarcity, or opportunity cost, or rationing device or any of a score of other myths woven by capitalistic economics, he cannot, in good conscience, agree to abolish interest. Zero rate of interest, therefore, is completely unacceptable. Only a new form or a new meaning or at the most a new name is to be given to interest. The bitter pill will stay, only some form of acceptable sugar-coating deserves to be invented.

Let us illustrate the difficulty by referring to a couple of excellent books on Islamic economics written by some of the most competent of Islamic economists. Enormously valuable material is available in both the books, except when they come to the issue of interest. Dr. 'Umer Chapra is very clear about prohibition of interest in Islam. He writes that "the nature of the prohibition of interest is strict, absolute and unambiguous."[100] When we come to brass tacks, the book becomes a carbon copy of any capitalistic economics text book. According to him "Low interest rates penalise savers ... contribute to inequalities... stimulate borrowing for consumption... generate inflationary pressure... stimulate unproductive investment and speculation... distorting the price of capital... reduce the gross savings ratio... and create capital shortages. Therefore cherished equilibrium, whereby interest rates would be neither high nor low, is just a theorctician's dream."[101] Some of these obstacles we have examined above and found untenable, some we will look into in the next few chapters and some, in fact, can be disproved from the invaluable wealth of material provided in his own book. But the point is that so far as we continue subscribing to the "kindergarten stories" spun out by capitalistic economics, we cannot make any creative contribution to Islamic economics. The end result of all the exceptionally valuable intellectual effort is that the Word of God which was confessedly "strict, absolute and unambiguous" is drowned in a whirlpool of the balderdash of capitalistic economics.

Four distinguished Pakistani economists led by Syed

Nawab Haider Naqvi have produced a monograph under the title of *Principles of Islamic Economic Reform*. It is an off-handish work shorn of serious deliberation of the cardinal issue of interest. Nevertheless, as one had a right to expect from the scholarship of the authors, they make some valuable observations. One of the most penetrating of them is that "Islamic rejection of interest is in effect a rejection of the entire capitalistic system: and interest-free economy is in fact an expolitation-free economy."[102] Although it is by no means a new contribution, it is well-worth repeating. It is also true that this will involve extensive land reforms,[103] another point which also stands conceded, at least by almost all socially responsive Islamists and Islamic economists. Do we then proceed to abolish interest in this wide meaning and also institute *zakat* in an equally wide meaning given to it by Caliph Umar and Caliph Ali? The authors' reply is an emphatic no. If attempts are "made to achieve these targets... irrespective of their effects on the economy ... nothing could be more dangerous."[104]

According to the authors, the "entire purpose of the Islamization process ... is to usher in a society based on *al-'adl* and *al-ihsan*".[105] True, these are *policy objectives* of Islam, but these are not its *policy instruments*. *'Adl* is unavoidably linked with extinction of exploitation represented by interest, just as *ihsan* represents eradication of want subsumed under the nomenclature of *zakat*. Since both have been declared "dangerous", we have a right to enquire why. About *zakat* there is complete silence. About interest, the book is fairly vocal. Opportunity cost of capital has to stay,[106] it is necessary to encourage savings in an inflationary situation,[107] and scarcity value of capital has to be paid.[108] As we have already seen above, these assertions do not have an iota of substance in them. Yet it is on these shibboleths that the authors reach the decision that "it is meaningless even to talk of a zero rate of interest."[109] The nearest they can come to elimination of interest is to change its name to indexation.[110] As if we were short of notions in self-deception and subterfuge!

There is however one extremely penetrating observation worth the value of the whole book. They write: "There is no way to replace interest on an economy-wide basis unless the process of monetary creation is directly linked to the process of production, and both the saving and investment activities are co-ordinated."[111] They, however, are incorrect in regarding this to be possible only if the public sector becomes the sole saver and investor. In the model of interest-free banking being presented in the next chapter both these conditions will be met in the context of free enterprise. It is also the contention of the present writer that these essential conditions can be met only in the context of an interest-free economy. The reason is that it is only after extinction of interest that it becomes possible to ensure equality between saving and investment at the ex-ante level. The equality between the two supposed to be attainable at the ex-post level is completely devoid of meaning. Like tomorrow, ex-post is something we never experience.

There are two statements in the monograph in which the learned authors are factually incorrect. They state that profits tend to grow at a rate faster than wages,[112] and that profits and rents are far more exploitative than interest.[113] None of the observations made by the learned authors is supported by objective reality. Looking up relevant figures from *National Income and Product Accounts of United States*, 1929-74 (pp 36-37) and the subsequent edition for years 1976-79 (P.7), both published by U.S. Department of Commerce, Washington, D.C., for a period of 31 years, from 1949 to 1979, we find that while the national income rose by 823%, wages rose by 933%, proprietor's income by 264%, rental income by 399%, corporate profits by 630%, net interest spurted by 6468%. No error here, the figure is six thousand four hundred and sixty eight per cent. This shows that while national income rose somewhat more than 8 times in 31 years, net interest income rose more than 64 times during the same time-span. Conversely in comparison with the percentage of rise in national income proprietor's income, rental income, and corporate profits have all suffered a comparative shortfall in the pace of growth, varying from 24.45% in the case of corporate profits to 67.92% in the case of proprietor's income. This means that every part of the two observations made by the learned authors is the exact reverse of reality.

Errors of this nature are particularly regrettable as these can lead to far-reaching theoretical and policy implications. This also shows that capitalistic economics alone does not live on shibboleths; socialistic and even some pseudo-liberal versions of economics also subsist on slogans. Islamic economics will come into its own only when it learns to outgrow these shibboleths and slogans and relates itself meaningfully to objective realities of economic life.

If Islamic economists do not know how to evolve an unexploitative substitute of interest, they should admit it, instead of saying that interest cannot be abolished. By making the latter statement, they imply that the fault is not with their creative capabilities but with the Word of Allah which demands something impossible of attainment.

CHAPTER – II
Interest -- Free Banking Structure

Whither Do We Go?

It has to be conceded that the background is substantially sombre. It is obvious that we can hardly derive any guidance from it regarding how to eliminate interest. All versions of economics, at least at their best, including capitalistic, socialistic and Islamic concur that interest should be abolished, but leaving aside various guiles and subterfuges there is not a single ray of light on how to devise a banking structure on zero rate of interest, or to put it in the language of Keynes, how to attain "euthanasia of the rentier."

We might perhaps go to Iqbal who gave us the vision and the inspiration for the creation of this country, founded on his conviction that Islamic ideology is capable of providing "provision honourable" to man, which, from a scientific point of view, is not possible without extinction of interest, precisely the thing about whose mode of attainement we are signally unaware. Iqbal is not the one who will relinquish any of his responsibilities. In a plight like the one we are in, his reply is as under, given in his *Javid Nama*,

Ma'nye tazah ke jo'aymo nayabaim kujast
Masjido maktabo maykhana 'aqeem und hama
Harfe az khaishtan a'mozo deran harf besoze
Ke dareen khankah bey soze kaleem und hama

The meanings new I seek
Where shall I find and sing?
The pub, the mosque, the school
Bare, barren is their spring.
Learn from thyself, and let
That word thy being claim,

For in this monastery
Like Moses none's aflame[114]

If we turn to Iqbal again saying that we do not know even that word to which, if we dedicated ourselves, we could secure release from the stranglehold of money, he replies as under:

Az riba akhar cheh mee zaid? fitan
Kas na danad lazzati qarz-i-hasan

What usury breeds save tension all around?
Of the bliss of noble lending none's aware.

Here, the expression *qarz-i-hasan* has been translated as "noble lending". So Iqbal's reply is to concentrate on *qarz-i-hasan,* which basically means a loan without interest or in scientific terminology a loan at zero rate of interest. How to evolve a banking system on the basis of zero rate of interest is precisely the thing of which we are unaware. We approach Iqbal again to give us at least a pointer, a king-pin or a foundation stone on which we may be able to raise a new banking edifice, at zero rate of interest. His answer is time. Make time the lever of your mechanism and you will be able to devise a banking structure which is shorn of the depredation of interest. In *Javid Nama* again, he makes Zarwan, the spirit of time, deliver a long oration, whose substance is that nothing creative or destructive is beyond its reach. In part, Zarwan proclaims:

Basta har tadbeer ba taqdeer-e-mun
Natiq-o-samit hama nakhcheer-e-mun
Ghuncha andar shakh mee balad ze mun
Murghak andar ashian nalad ze mun
Dana az parwaz-e-man gardad nihal
Har firaq az faiz-e-man gardad wisal
Ham itabe ham khitabe awaram
Tishna sazam ta sharabe awaram

"All efforts are related to my fate
I have thus enslaved the eloquent, the mute,
For me the beauteous bud upon the branch
Doth bloom, and sings the bird in nest. I fly
And give its growth to grain, with union crown
The lover's separation. I rebuke
And I reward: I cause the pangs of thirst
Until I bring the wine."

When Iqbal projects time as a massive and pervasive force a question naturally arises in mind whether we cannot get its help in providing us with our basis of banking. When we think of the fact that time is as much an inescapable ingredient of a loan as money itself, diverse tantalizing possibilities start glimmering before our eyes. Zarwan claims, "I cause the pangs of thirst until I bring the wine." The problem of substitution of interest involves solving the problem of time. This thirst has been there for four thousand years. But where is the wine? That too only time can deliver. So, the reply of Iqbal appears to be that if we utilize time as the main lever of our banking mechanism, we may be able to reach our goal of interest-free banking mechanism.

Obstacles in The Way

Before we follow the guidance of Iqbal, let us list all the obstacles that we will be called upon to negotiate while building our model of interest-free banking.

1. Even after receiving guidance from Iqbal regarding building our model on the basis of time, we are still far from building it. Building a model and knowing its basic ingredient are two different things. So the first problem of replacing interest by time is the operative pattern of the model.

2. Even if we succeed in evolving such a model, a foundational question will be whether savings will continue to be generated. What assurance is there that despite lowering interest to zero, savings will not slacken?

3. Even if this assurance is available both in irrefutable logic and unquestionable empirical evidence, it does not follow that savings will continue to be attracted by banks which pay no interest on deposits. The presumption appears to be that they will not. This presumption needs to be evaluated and catered for.

4. Assuming we cross the first three hurdles, one thing is certain beyond dispute, *viz.*, the demand for loans will outstrip by a large margin the supply of loans . Any model which fails to meet this problem will not be workable .

It is true that the banking structure as constituted , artificially restricts the supply of loans , through the institution of bank reserve. It is also true that much manipulation is possible in this area to meet the obstacle raised by this problem . If we go to the logical limit to ensure that the inordinate rise in the demand of loans at zero rate of interest is met by an equally inordinate rise in the supply of loans , it can become necessary for us to throw overboard the entire concept of statutory reserve.

5. Just as it is not possible to introduce interest-free banking without devising an interest-free mechanism, similarly extinction of statutary reserve is not possible without evolving an equally effective liquidity mechanism.

6. This arrangement of bank liquidity should be an intrinsic part of the model, and not foisted on it from outside its own being, like deposit insurance or government or central bank backing.

7. Supposing we cross all the six hurdles, the question arises whether this inordinate expansion of credit matched by an equivalent supply of credit will not push the price level in the inflationary direction. Avoiding this will obviously involve rigorous credit control denying credit to all consumptional, speculative and fiscal deficit covering loans.

8. This in turn involves the issue whether this can be done, when all over the world, government deficit is increasingly appropriating inordinate proportion of lending resources.

Unless the model has an in-built arrangement whereby we can be reasonably assured that the induction of interest-free banking is capable of solving the problem of fiscal deficit, the model will not remain workable.

9. After extinction of both interest and statutary reserve, we must face the problem of monetary control mechanism. How is the interest-free model to face this issue?

10. Will such a banking which pays no interest on deposits and claims no interest on advances be at all profitable? Because, unless it is profitable, private enterprise will not enter this sector which means we will be writing off efficient and progressive functioning of the banking sector.

These are the ten major issues which any induction of interest-free banking has to face. In all humility, the present writer begs leave to answer these problems, and leave it to the discerning reader to decide whether the issues have been adequately resolved. The exposition that follows sticks to the order in which these problems have been posed.

Time as The Basis of Interest-Free Banking

Once we come to note that time is as much an ingredient of a loan as the loan itself, only a little concentration persuades us to evolve the concept of loan value. What the lender foregoes and the borrower receives is not merely an amount of loan, but an amount of loan *for a certain period of time*. If we multiply the amount of loan by the period for which it is advanced, we get the measure of deprivation suffered by the lender which is also the measure of gain received by the borrower. It is this magnitude that we may call by the name of loan value. To illustrate this concept, we may say that the following loans have exactly identical loan values:

Rs. 1,000 for one year
Rs. 500 for two years
Rs. 250 for four years
Rs. 200 for five years
Rs. 100 for ten years

If these loan values are exactly identical, then we have a foundational notion for the evolution of interest-free banking. Every borrower should exchange equivalent loan values with the bank. He may give to the bank only a fraction of the loan that he receives, but advance it for such a multiple of time that equivalent loan values are exchanged between the bank and the borrower. What should be a suitable fraction of loan and a suitable multiple of time for which a counter-loan should be given in exchange for every loan, is a point which the monetary policy of any country, accepting this basis of banking, will decide according to the exigencies of a given situation.

For purposes of illustrating the concept, we are adopting 12-1/2 % as the measure of counter-loan, which by necessity implies 8 multiples of the time-period for which a loan is received. So the formula we are adopting is that Rs. 1,000 for one year has the same loan value as Rs. 125 for eight years. Let a borrower of Rs. 1000 for one year from the bank, pay to the bank a counter loan of Rs. 125 for eight years, and both parties will have exchanged equivalent loan values. At the end of one year, the borrower will return his loan of Rs. 1000 to the bank without the addition of any kind of excess, and he or his dependents will receive back Rs. 125 at the end of eight years, likewise without the addition of any interest.

If the borrower cannot return the amount within one year, he can renew the agreement for the loan, let us say for another year, by either giving another Rs. 125 for eight years, or extending the period of deposit of his original Rs. 125 from eight to sixteen years.

The real test whether a genuinely workable alternative to interest has been found or not is to ask whether this alternative has an in-built capacity to encash premature commercial bills at face value. Let us assume that monetary authority has fixed 12-1/2 % as the level of counter-loan. Now, if a commercial paper worth Rs. 10,000 is to be encashed, and this bill is short of maturity by 30 days, this means accommodation of the loan value of 300,000 units (10,000 x 30 days) is needed. The bill can be encashed at par, provided the owner of the bill gives a counter loan of Rs. 1,250 for 240 days. 1,250 multiplied by 240 also means 300,000 units of loan value. It is through this exchange of equivalent loan values that any commercial paper for any period short of maturity can be encashed at par. All attempts for eliminating interest foundered on the intractability of the problem of encashment of pre-mature commercial paper. Hitherto Islamic economics, like identical versions of Judaism and Christianity before it, has been forced to devise subterfuges which tended in effect to perpetuate interest. Now that we have a genuine alternative to interest, necessity for retaining this exploitative institution ceases to exist, and a cease-fire with Allah and His Apostle becomes possible.

This must be pointed out that though lending on the basis of time will be completely free of interest, the viability of the banking structure can be threatened if loans are advanced without collateral. It is suggested that a collateral of 110 per cent of the loan should be demanded for all loans. The exact level that should be fixed at a particular time and place is for the monetary authority to determine.

So, we have crossed the first of the ten hurdles in the way of evolving an interest-free banking model. Iqbal's guidance to establish *qarz-i-hasan,* with the help of time, has come to assume a specific and concrete form. The name by which this model has come to be called is Time-Multiple Counter-Loan (TMCL) basis.

Whether Savings Will Slacken in Interest-Free Banking

If reason and empirical evidence have any bearing on reaching a decision regarding the impact on saving of abolition of interest, it is possible to prove that savings will not only not fall, but will tend to rise significantly after abolition of interest.

It is true that pre-Keynesian economics held the opposite view, and some watered-down expression of this view can be met on occasion even now. But the finality with which Keynes repudiated the argument of classicists regarding direct relationship of savings with interest remains unanswered to this day. Keynes argued that the lower the rate of interest, the higher the level of investments, therefore higher the level of employment, therefore higher the level of incomes, and therefore higher the level of savings,[115] This means, Keynes maintains, that the highest level of savings can only be obtained at the lowest level of interest. In point of logic not a single step of the argument of Keynes can be repudiated, and therefore his conclusion remains unassailed to this day. Yet academic and professional bias, already discussed, has not liked to permit logic to prevail.

Empirical proof supports this contention of Keynes with no less vehemence. It is true that no country had a zero rate of interest from which to get figures. But there is a concept in economics which is called real rate of interest. Real rate means interest rate minus the rate of inflation, so that a negative real rate is possible when the rate of inflation exceeds the interest rate. During the recent past, it happened with considerable frequency, permitting us to examine its results.

The present writer collected figures of bank deposits of five countries, *viz.*, U.K., Germany, Japan, Switzerland and U.S.A. for every year of the decade of the seventies.[116] Real rate of interest is a negative entity in U.K. and Germany in 6 years out of 10, in Japan in 9 years out of 10, in Switzerland in 8 years out of 10, and in U.S.A. in 4 years out of 10, yet the rise in total deposits of banks continued in all these years, without exhibiting any relationship with negative real rate of interest in any of these countries.[117] Even when negative real rate rose to a double digit level as in Japan (1974: minus 15.33 per cent), in Great Britain (1975: minus 12.97 per cent), and almost so in U.S.A. (1974: minus 9.86 per cent), the accretion in bank deposits continued uninterrupted. In these countries during these double digit years, bank deposits, far from falling, rose by 10.87 per cent, 5.72 per cent and 9.43 per cent respectively,[118] completely demolishing deposit mobilization capability assigned to interest.

In this exercise, out of 50 period-countries 49 show complete unconcern with the rate of interest in the matter of bank deposits which keep rising from year to year. The only single exception is West Germany and the year is 1979. Bank deposits fell in this year by 12.08 per cent. This exceptional occurrence directly supports inverse relationship between interest and saving, espoused by Keynes. Bank rate in West Germany was 3 per cent in 1978 and was doubled in 1979 to 6 per cent,[119] and that explains the fall in incomes, the fall in savings, and therefore the fall in bank deposits.

In fact, we do not need to go to West Germany to measure the adverse impact of interest on savings. The experience of Pakistan is far more dramatic and far more compelling. According to World Bank statistics gross domestic savings in Pakistan were 13 per cent in 1965 and dwindled to 5 per cent in 1985.[120] The reason is obvious. The bank rate was 5% in 1965 and was 10% in 1985. Loans could be had at about 9% in 1965, these could not be raised for much less than 18% in 1985. Therefore savings have dwindled from 13% to 5%. If we want to revert to the level of savings of 1965, we have only to revert to the bank rate and loan rate levels of 1965. If we want a yet higher level of saving, we need to lower interest even beyond the one obtaining in 1965.

So, the second hurdle to the induction of interest-free banking is merely a myth woven by classical economics. If logic and empirical evidence have any validity, there is not an iota of doubt that highest possible savings must occur at zero rate of interest.

Savings Must Come to Interest-Free Banks

Prima facie, there appears substance in the argument that, even conceding inverse relationship between interest and saving, it does not follow that at zero rate of interest savings must necessarily take the shape of bank deposits. It appears plausible that many savers instead of putting their money in a current deposit (for all deposits become current deposits in interest-free banks) may choose to invest it in a rent-yielding or a profit-yielding asset. In fact, many people who are earning interest on their deposits at present, on the introduction of interest-free banking, may hasten to invest their assets in the purchase of land or houses or stock exchange shares, perhaps even gold.

All this is substantially correct, but the conclusion that this can or will have any adverse impact on the magnitude of bank deposits is by and large incorrect. Let us take an example. Supposing a saving bank depositor, or an institution, whose sole income is constituted by the interest it earns on its deposits, finds itself forced to shift over to some rent-yielding or profit-yielding asset, before its deposit ceases to earn any interest. What will it do? Let us say, it will buy land or houses or shares on the stock exchange. But it can do so only if there is a matching seller. Therefore, whatever the number of depositors who want to shift from zero interest deposits to income-yielding assets must find sellers who want to dispose of these assets. As soon as a deal is completed, and whether the payment is made in the shape of a cheque or cash, the deposit of the seller is likely to increase, as a general rule, in the same measure in which the deposit of the purchaser is depleted.

This argument remains unimpaired if the seller in turn shifts to some other real investment, and the next seller does likewise and so on. Because at the end of the entire circuit, there is bound to be a seller who needs to deposit his money in the bank from the considerations of safe custody and convenience of a checking account. If in the entire circuit of purchases, every payment is made by cheque, as is likely, the money will stay as a deposit in the account of one or another of these various buyers and sellers, even during the entire period of these transactions.

We must not forget the fact that interest or no interest, money remains the hot potato in the children's game, which can come to rest only in a bank. Unless people start preferring stacking bundles of bank notes under their pillows, in preference to security of their money provided by bank deposits, and convenience of payment provided by cheque-books, lowering interest to zero cannot make any difference to the totality of deposits available to any banking system. The only difference eventually will be in the upward direction, on account of revolutionary expansion in investment, employment, income and saving, as direct consequence of extinction of interest.

This third hurdle in the path of interest-free banking also stands removed. Actually, the hurdle itself has no legs to stand upon. It is raised on the misappraisal of money (and bank deposit) being of the nature of a stock, whereas both are of the nature of a flow, so that whatever is taken out must irresistibly flow back to the bank, and make lending of an identical amount possible, unless self-imposed impediment of bank reserve is made to stand in the way.

Equilibrium Between Demand and Supply of Loans

This brings us to the fourth major obstacle regarding equilibrium between demand and supply of loans, that stands in the way of introduction of interest-free banking. Locke questioned advisability of lowering interest to even 4 per cent. "I have but this one short question to ask", he wrote addressing those who demanded lowering interest to 4 per cent, "will 4 per cent increase the number of lenders?"[121] So far as this writer is aware, this question remains unanswered to this day, unless we regard Keynesian inverse relationship between interest and saving to be an adequate reply to the penetrating question asked by Locke.

It must be conceded that this reply will not be adequate in the context of interest-free banking. The demand for loans will increase manifold *on the day* interest is reduced to zero, and the phenomenal increase in deposits as its consequence has yet to travel the road of increased investment, employment, incomes, savings and therefore bank deposits. All this belongs to *the day after*. What is there to cover the gap?

The distinguishing feature of every interest-oriented

banking structure in every country is the institution of bank reserve. Banks do not lend out all the money they receive in deposits; they retain a percentage as reserve. This percentage varies from country to country. In Pakistan it is 35 per cent. This means that an initial deposit of Rs. 100 can enable banks in Pakistan to advance initial loans not exceeding Rs. 65. However, since every loan advanced by a bank flows back into the banking system on account of derivative deposits, long before the borrower has paid back his loan, the bank can lend out these derivative deposits as well, after deducting the prescribed reserve in every turn over. It is possible to calculate the lending capacity of a banking structure by reference to its statutory reserve. Its lending capacity is the reciprocal of this reserve. At 35% statutory reserve, the one obtaining in Pakistan, the expansion of credit cannot exceed the reciprocal of 35% (*i.e.* 100÷35 = 2.85 multiples). If we lower the reserve to 25 per cent, we can advance 4 multiples of deposits, at 20% reserve, we can advance 5 multiples, at 10%, ten multiples, at 1% 100 multiples, and at zero reserve, infinite number of multiples.

This is not some kind of sleight of hand which produces these multiples, but is implicit in the fact that every advance of a loan by a bank, as a general rule, comes back to the banking system, no matter how the borrower spends his loan, in the form of one or more deposits, at the normal speed of velocity of money, long before the borrower returns his loan to the bank. It is therefore not correct to say that banks create credit out of thin air, howsoever much they may appear to be doing it. Their total assets (in the main loans) can never exceed their total liabilities (in the main deposits). At zero reserve, this fundamental position will not change. Even after obtaining capacity for infinite advancement of loans to meet infinite demand of loans, the equilibrium between assets and liabilities remains undisturbed.

Since the fourth hurdle to the introduction of interest-free banking demanded an in-built device in the model to strike an equilibrium between demand and supply of loans at zero rate of interest, we can achieve it by abolishing banking reserve altogether. This single device is capable of making the supply of loans to remain in *perpetual* equilibrium with the demand of loans, no matter what their magnitude.

Evaluation of Extinction of Statutory Reserve

Though the fourth hurdle to the introduction of interest-free banking stands removed, it has been removed by making a radical departure from the conventional concept of banking. It calls for a justification for making that departure in the light of evaluation of what we will lose and what we will gain.

We lose two things, *viz.*, liquidity of the entire banking system, and one of the monetary management mechanisms. It is conceded without any discussion that no viable banking system can afford to lose either of these. This does not amount to conceding that a substitution of these two functions is not possible. Just as abolition of interest is not possible without evolving an unexploitative but equally workable alternative to it, similarly abolition of statutory reserve is not possible without evolving an equally effective alternative to it.

Since liquidity mechanism that is proposed is the subject of point No. 5, and monetary control mechanism the subject of point No. 9 identified above under the title of "*Obstacles in the Way*", these will be expounded in that order, and the reader is requested to suspend his disbelief till he has evaluated the alternatives that the model provides so that no deprivation occurs in either of these two directions. Though, for purposes of precision and clarity, the substitutional device will be detailed after a while, two assurances can be given in advance. The substitutes for both the positive contributions of statutory reserve will be as effective as the ones provided by statutory reserve. Secondly, there will be no graft work. Nothing extraneous to TMCL concept will be called in to help support the model.

Statutory reserve does not only represent the two positive

implications already indicated; it involves several negative consequences as well. The negative consequences are the artificial injection of scarcity into the capital market, and making this the basic argument for perpetuation of interest. Now that we are trying to evolve interest-free banking, we cannot retain in our model the basic reason for the existence of interest, *viz*., scarcity of capital resources, artificially built into the system through this very statutory reserve. The relationship between statutory reserve and interest is the one between the invisible roots of a *sheesham* tree, and the visible parts of the tree. If we cut out a *sheesham* tree even six inches below the surface of the land, cover it up with earth, and run it over with a roller, the *sheesham* tree will start growing again. That is why TMCL model declines to make any compromise on this issue. We could have estimated the likely increase in demand for credit at, let us say, twenty multiples of deposits, on lowering interest to zero, and fixed 5% as bank reserve which would be eminently workable, as we will detail in the next section. But a situation can emerge in which demand for loans may increase to thirty multiples of deposits, and the monetary authority may hold the view that no further lowering of liquidity will be consistent with the over-all security of the banking system, with the result that no option will be left to it except to re-introduce interest. The model therefore holds that cutting out the *sheesham* tree is not enough, we must dig out all its roots as well.

The second important negative consequence of bank reserve is diverse varieties of disequilibria injected into our economy by the asymmetry between deposits and loans. Let us forget for a while the various multiples of *initial* deposits which a banking system can lend out up to the limit of reciprocal of statutory reserve. If we neglect for sometime the differentiation between initial and derivative deposits, and regard all kinds of deposits a single entity as any bank balance sheet does, the total advances of any bank, under statutory reserve, have perforce to be less than total deposits, whereas in contradistinction to it, all advances come back to the banking system, as a general rule, without suffering any deduction.

There is an obvious asymmetry in the arrangement. While all deposits must suffer some deduction before these become advances, all advances must come back to the banking system as deposits.

This unavoidable and in fact in-built asymmetry between deposits and advances has far-reaching implications with adverse consequences on the functioning of the entire economy. If we regard bank deposits as the main supply of savings of a people, and bank advances the main financial source of investments, this asymmetry means that investments must always fall short of saving which must by definition result in perpetuation of under-employment equilibrium. This means that unemployment which basically flows out of interest receives supporting intractability at the hands of statutory reserve. When incorrect analysis and mistaken medication, at the behest of "safe" and "sane" economists, pull us in the direction of consumptional expansionism, the mass of people start getting pulverized between the mill-stones of unemployment and inflation.

To sum up, even if we overlook the necessity of the proposed banking model to generate adequate supply of capital to strike an equilibrium with the demand for capital at zero rate of interest, there are weightier fundamental reasons why statutory reserve should be done away with. Its main positive contribution of liquidity of the banking sector has to be, and can be as we shall soon see, catered for in some other way. But its negative afflictions, *viz.*,artificial injection of scarcity in the supply of capital, and an equally built-in asymmetry between deposits and advances, which eventually means asymmetry between savings and investment, possess such deeply despoiling consequences, that we must look around for some method of getting rid of it.

Alternative to Bank Reserve

This brings us to the fifth major obstacle to the introduction of interest-free banking. If the need of equilibrium between demand and supply of loans at zero rate of interest calls for extinction of statutory reserve, we have to devise an alternative mechanism for ensuring liquidity of the banking sector.

It so happens that TMCL concept is entirely capable of meeting this demand. If we closely look into the potentialities of this concept, we find that it is not only capable of providing us with a feasible alternative to interest, it has the potential of furnishing us with an equally humane and unconstrictive alternative to bank reserve. Let us suppose that monetary authority in a particular economic environment has fixed 12 1/2 per cent as the level of counter loan. This means that a borrower from a bank will need to furnish to it as counter loan 12-1/2 per cent of the amount of the loan that he needs, for eight multiples of the period for which he requires the loan.

There is every reason for us to extend this concept from the area of borrowers and banks to that of banks and the central bank. The banks can be required to deposit with the central bank 2-1/2 percentage points of the counter loans they receive, which makes them eligible to secure interest-free advances of upto 8 multiples of their respective deposits with the central bank. This provides every bank with a liquidity of 2-1/2 x 8 = 20 per cent of its total liabilities. Besides 2 percentage points of all counter loans will be retained by the bank as till money. This furnishes the banking houses with a total liquidity of 22 per cent of all their liabilities, without vitiating the principle of consistent equilibrium between deposits and advances which we will have already achieved by elimination of bank reserve.

It is true that this does not work up to 35% bank reserve at present obtaining in Pakistan. By raising the percentage of counter-loan, it is entirely possible to reach that level as well. But that level would be substantially over-fixed, and is entirely unnecessary, particularly under the banking model which is being presented, which has the inherent capability of providing both growth and stability to any economy which works on it. Once cyclical nature of growth is exorcized from the economy, which is one of the major contributions of elimination of interest and statutory reserve, the need to revert to liquidity itself becomes substantially remote.

Goldsmith establishments, from which modern banking evolved, originally worked on the basis of 100 per cent reserve.[122] This ratio, notwithstanding fluctuations in the course of history, has tended to fall over the long haul, till we reach the present U.S. level on different varieties of deposits ranging from 3 to 16-1/2%.[123] Samuelson records the argument of bankers "that legal reserves of as little as 10 per cent – some of us would say 5 per cent – are all that prudence requires in this age of insured deposits".[124] So far as till money is concerned, according to Samuelson, "perhaps less than 2 per cent normally seems needed in the form of cash".[125]

Twenty-two per cent should therefore be regarded adequate liquidity, but the model is capable of giving higher or lower liquidity as may be demanded by any monetary authority. In any case, the fifth hurdle to the introduction of interest-free banking stands removed.

Endogenous Nature of Liquidity Arrangement

It was demanded from the model that it should provide liquidity from within its own being, without calling for any help from concepts like deposit insurance, central bank backing or government support.

Although while crossing over the fifth obstacle, this sixth demand has been met in its entirety, we cannot completely neglect the modern concepts of banking as these are developing in the world around us. These concepts have a substantial bearing on the question of liquidity.

To begin with, there has been significant evolution in the concept and practice of bankers bank. Writes Karunatilake, "In a banking system with a central bank, itself capable of creating money to act as lender of the last resort, the function of bank reserves as cushion of liquidity is no longer important."[126] This lender of last resort assurance makes a large part of reserves as redundant, so far as the original purpose of reserves is concerned. This is the more so because the governments now stand behind the banks more than these ever did before. According to Samuelson, if a banking panic were to occur in U.S.A. once again, "Congress, the President and the Federal Reserve Board would all act, even using their constitutional powers over money to print the money needed to meet a national emergency"[127] The measure in which governmental backing imparts confidence would be clear from a single example. The federal deposit insurance agencies have resources of less than 1% of the deposits they have insured,[128] and yet the confidence generated by governmental involvement has not yet proved the resources inadequate.

Besides the development of the concept of bankers bank, along with concern and backing of the government, the development of deposit insurance has also worked in the same direction. In U.S.A. Federal Deposit Insurance Scheme covers all deposits up to the first 100,000 dollars and this has prevented bank failures and panic.[129] In the evaluation of Samuelson in future banks will be closed by bank examiners and government authorities and not by the panicky behaviour of depositors. He points out that in the 1970s the only banks that failed were those involved in fraud or gross negligence, but their depositors were protected by the FDIC.[130]

There is nothing in TMCL concept that conflicts with any of these developments in the concept of banking. Yet it does not lean on any of these concepts for the assurance of its liquidity which is in-built in the model itself.

The model can therefore rightly claim to have crossed over the sixth hurdle in the way of introduction of interest-free banking.

How to Control Inflationary Pressure Implicit in the Model?

The seventh hurdle which the model must of necessity cross is that of inflationary pressures that must accompany inordinate expansion of credit. Since the demand for credit at zero rate of interest is bound to be inordinately large which will not be obstructed because of equally inordinate supply of credit owing to the elimination of bank reserve, the pressure on the price level is bound to become irresistible, falsifying the entire creativity which the model, but for this grave shortcoming, may have generated.

This objection assumes that under TMCL banking every demand for loan, subject only to provision of counter loan and adequate collateral will be granted. It is true that the model is entirely capable of doing it, but it must decline to do it. It is workable only subject to rigorous credit control. All requests for productive loans whether pertaining to agriculture, or industry or trade will be granted. All non-productive loans whether related to consumptional or speculative or even government deficit covering purposes will be denied.

It is conceded that this last category of exclusion is beyond the competence of banking sector and even the monetary authority to dictate. It is also conceded that considering the fact that more than half the loanable resources in the entire so-called free-world are taken away by the governments of these countries to meet the essential requirements of running these countries and this percentage is consistently rising, workability of this exclusion appears contestable. Again, this is an issue which is the very next we are taking up and must therefore seek the indulgence of the critical reader, in the interest of clarity of exposition, to confine to the issue whether or not inflation can or cannot be kept under control, within the parameters of the model.

One essential parameter of the model is acceptance of all requests for productive loans and denial of all requests for non-productive ones. What the model aims at is to exclude consumptional expansionism which has been operative throughout the world, ever since the end of World War II, and inflicting virtually unending inflation on it. Since expansionism is to continue if we wish to give employment to all, the model provides productive expansionism in place of consumptional expansionism. Far from leading to inflation, it should provide assurance of stability.

It can be argued that the vast expansion of credit, even though confined to productive area, can yet be inflationary because of time-lag between the extension of credit and the production of goods and services capable of absorbing the increased money supply. This objection overlooks the existence of idle capacity, and the impact that lowering interest by stages to zero will have on the activation of this capacity. In the industrialized countries, this capacity is regarded close to 20 per cent.[131] In Pakistan, with a rate of interest generally higher than most industrialized countries, idle installed capacity appears close to 25 per cent. As we lower by steps, the interest rate and the reserve level, a point relating to strategy and dealt with in the next chapter, not only new capacity is installed, but idle capacity is also quickened to life. This activation of idle capacity is entirely capable of covering the time gap till successively increasing flow of productive loans reaches its respective fruition, obliterating the impact of time-lag.

Another factor which deserves to be kept in view in this context is the remarkable capacity of the banking model under discussion of contracting credit in a measure equal to the creation of credit by extension of loans. Every loan is matched by an *equivalent* counter-loan. Even though this counter-loan may be a fraction of the loan advanced, the period of availability of the former, as we have already seen, will be a matching multiple of the latter, so that loan values advanced and claimed are exactly equal. This arrangement will prove to be yet another contributory factor to impart stability to the price level, despite all the growth which is implicit in the model.

TMCL banking is therefore entirely capable of crossing the seventh hurdle which appears to stand in the way of interest-free banking, though some subsidiary issues need further looking into.

What About Consumptional Loans?

A critic may find fault with the model pointing his accusing finger at the apparent impotency of the model to meet consumptional requirements. Actually TMCL concept, *per se,* is neutral to the purpose for which a loan is sought. Whether a loan is needed for a productive purpose, a speculative purpose, a consumptional purpose or for fighting a war, it can be secured, at the theoretical level at least, under this arrangement. The reason for excluding, in the exposition of the concept, the last three varieties of loans is to avoid the inflationary possibilities that expansion of credit for these purposes can generate, and not for any inherent impossibility of advances for these purposes.

A few facts in connection with consumptional loans need to be kept in view, in this context. Firstly, the need for consumptional loan in the capitalistic system is largely dictated by the incapacity of purchasing power to keep pace with the productive capability of the system. Leakage of purchasing power occurs primarily in the process of fattening the rentier, with identical impulses extending from interest to rent and profit levels. This cumulative exploitation makes labourers incapable of purchasing goods which they themselves produce. With the introduction of interest-free banking not only leakage dictated by the rentier will suffer extinction, its extension in the areas of rent and profit will cease to exist. The consequence will be that Say's Law, which postulates supply creating its own demand, will become operative, excluding the basic compulsion of the economy to resort to consumptional loans.

Secondly, it is not necessary that all varieties of consumptional loans may be excluded from the ambit of the model for all time. It is a precaution necessary for the initial years. When functioning of interest-free banking for a few years confirms the promise of the model to maintain stability of the price level, we can lower our guard and include some, or several, varieties of consumptional loans in the area of its operation. In that case, we shall rely on the enormous resilience of every economy to take on this fractional additional burden.

What Would Happen in The Case of War?

There is nothing in the TMCL concept which excludes or reduces the capability of any government for borrowing from the money market. Counter loans will generate loans for fighting a war just as they do so for productive purposes.

We must remember that it is the intra-national distortions of the economy which create the necessity of international exploitation which in turn becomes the main propeller of all wars. The fact is that international conflicts and tensions are a mere projection of internal conflicts and tensions, spawned by exploitation of capital in the capitalist countries, and that of the monolithic state in socialist ones. The capitalist countries perpetually suffer from unemployment, which these must strive to export to weaker countries, and the socialist ones suffer no less from under-production, both quantitative and qualitative, on account of loss of initiative and enterprise, consequent on extinction of profit motive. Both must therefore cover their internal weakness by the colossal build-up of their war machines. If these countries could give bread with dignity and freedom to their people, hectic preparations for war would no longer be necessary.

Whichever country in the world introduces interest-free banking first of all will become the first one in history capable of giving assurance both of worthwhile employment and of freedom to its people, releasing them at once from the demeaning dole of western democracies, even more demeaning restrictive practices of socialist countries, and far more demeaning privation of the masses in the Third World. Once a country adopts the way to the conferment of the Quranic ideal of *rizkun kareem*[132] on its people, the way itself will become so much worth fighting for that the defence potential of the nation is likely to rise by several multiples, without adding a single gun or a single soldier to its fighting forces.

Though the chances of such a country being dragged

into a war diminish corresponding to this accretion of strength, this in itself provides no guarantee that war will not be foisted on it. If it has to fight a war, it will raise finances in the same way as is conventionally done at present, except borrowing on interest. It will postpone or curtail consumption, raise taxes and borrow money on counter-loan basis.

In this respect, we could conceivably go beyond the TMCL concept to find resources to meet the cost of a prolonged war. It is emphasized that this observation may not be deemed to be a necessary ingredient of the model which is capable of standing on its own feet under all eventualities. However, it is a fundamental cultural consideration to give some thought to our present interest-oriented financial arrangements for fighting a war. It is only through interest-free banking, and perhaps even going somewhat beyond it, that the atrocious nature of these arrangements can be called to a halt. After all, it is both men and money that are needed to prosecute a war. Yet our distorted sense of values is reflected by the fact that whereas men can be conscripted to fight a war, money cannot be. The result is that loan capital emerges as the sole beneficiary of a war in which men wither and die, but money blooms and prospers. This reflects that supremacy of money over man which is the nadir of our cultural perversity, deserving complete obliteration, even apart from the economic compulsion to liberate man from the scourges of unemployment and inflation through abolition of interest. Therefore, continuation of interest-free banking, even during war, is the minimum response with which we can snatch sovereignty from the hands of money, and return it to man who far more eminently deserves to possess it.

If inflation emerges during war, as is likely, it will be because of the war, and not because of the TMCL concept.

Can The Model Achieve Fiscal Balance?

The eighth hurdle which the model must show itself

capable of crossing is to indicate the mechanism, and an in-built mechanism at that, by which it can confer capability of achieving balanced budgets on the fiscal authorities. This mechanism is doubly decisive because the model crossed over the seventh hurdle, the one relating to inflation, in the face of expansionary credit, by introducing selective credit control and declining to advance credit for any non-productive purpose including loans to cover fiscal deficit of governments.

Since this is the single largest chunk of credit which all banking systems in the so-called free world are obliged to advance, the self-confessed incapability of the model to advance this credit can render the entire model unworkable, unless it can fulfil its promise to impart redundancy to budgetary imbalance.

The model appears capable of accepting this responsibility on account of the fact that interest-free banking has the potential of making such extraordinary impact on both sides of the budgetary balance sheet and, to such an extent, that budgetary balance becomes an in-built consequence of the introduction of this model. To achieve this result, interest-free banking relies almost exclusively on the elimination of unemployment which among its numerous consequences dramatically raises budgetary receipts on the one side and significantly reduces government expenditure on the other, excluding the necessity of budgetary deficit. It is conceded that even under interest-free regime frictional unemployment will survive but its magnitude is unlikely to exceed 0.5%. This is proved by the World War experience of countries like England and U.S.A. where unemployment fell to this level. Switzerland, by consistently following a low interest rate policy (average bank rate during 35 years period from 1949 to 1983 has been 2.63 per cent),[133] had an average unemployment of 0.4 per cent during the decade of the seventies.[134] Frictional unemployment under interest-free regime therefore is unlikely to exceed 0.5 per cent.

To work out the budgetary impact of elimination of

unemployment, we need to take up a specific country and its budget in a specific year with as high a budgetary deficit as we can find, and calculate what impact a zero interest regime would have made to balance it in that year. Pakistan is as good a country as any other in the matter of intractibility of budgetary deficit, and the year 1986-87, the latest for which necessary figures are available, and also the one which had the highest deficit till that time, provides a fair enough basis for testing the impact of interest-free banking on erasing fiscal deficit.

According to the Annual Report of State Bank of Pakistan for the year 1986-87 (P. 154), the consolidated budgetary receipts of the Federal and Provincial Governments for the year 1986-87 were Rs. 99.55 billion, the total expenditure was Rs. 155.98 billion and the total deficit was Rs. 53.64 billion, after excluding Rs. 2.78 billion available as surplus of autonomous bodies. The revenue receipts formed 16.5 per cent of Gross Domestic Product, and the deficit formed 8.8 per cent of G.D.P. If we neither increase taxes nor reduce expenditure the only method left to erase this deficit is to increase the G.D.P. The measure of necessary increase is reached through dividing the deficit percentage by the revenue percentage and multiplying it by 100. The result we reach is (8.8÷16.5 x 100) 53.33 per cent. The critical test for the workability of TMCL model is whether or not it can erase fiscal deficit of this magnitude by increasing G.D.P. by something like 53.33 per cent, so that no reason is left for the government to make a demand on bank resources for covering its fiscal shortfall. It is a tall order and yet the model exhibits complete competence to meet it.

This competence emerges from the incapability of either unemployment or under-employment to survive under a credit structure willing and capable of advancing credit to all productive ventures, without making demand of interest. We now need to know two things, *viz.*,the measure of unemployment and under-employment that existed in Pakistan during the financial year 1986-87, and the difference that fall of each percentage point in unemployment makes towards increase in national income.

The figures for unemployment for Pakistan and other Third World countries are often undependable and imprecise. I.L.O. Yearbook provides no help as figures given in it relate to those who register their names in employment exchanges, which is not often done in Pakistan. *Pakistan Economic Survey,* dated by about two years, gives the figure of 4 per cent for unemployment but adds that "under-employment accounts for one-fourth of the employed persons."[135] This means that besides 4 per cent who are unemployed, 24 per cent are under-employed. The measure of their under-employment is not given. In such a case we can only apply rule of the thumb, and assume that the under-employed remain unemployed for an average of half of their working days. We get support for this assumption by the consideration that the bulk of 70.03 million of the population which lives in rural areas, out of the total population of 97.67 million (both estimates for 1985-86)[136] depends on agriculture and is generally idle for five months in the year. From this point of view, under-employment of 24% appears an under-estimate. It would therefore be fairly safe to regard 24 per cent under-employment to be equal to 12 per cent unemployment. Adding this 12% to 4% of conceded unemployment, we get a total unemployment figure of 16 per cent for Pakistan for the year 1984-85.

However, interest (*alias* mark-up) has tended to creep up from 17% in 1984-85 to 18% in 1986-87. If at 17% interest unemployment was 16%, at 18%, it should be nearer 17%. This is empirically supported by the deteriorating law and order situation in the country. This is further supported by particular intensification of this situation in Sind where the average of unemployment appears higher compared to other provinces because of the more stay-at-home temperament of our Sindhi brothers.

Whatever the reasons, the fact remains that in the year of reference, unemployment was fairly close to 17 per cent, but to take a conservative line, we shall treat it as 16 per cent, the one that obtained two years before *i.e.* in 1984-85.

Let us therefore say that in 1986-87, unemployment in Pakistan was of the level of 16 per cent, and since frictional unemployment of 0.5 per cent is not curable, therefore induction of interest-free banking could only cure 15.5 per cent of the unemployment that existed in that year. It is now left for us to measure the magnitude of the result on G.N.P., as a consequence of elimination of unemployment.

Fortunately, we do not have to undertake any theoretical exercise in the matter. Professor Arthur M. Okun has already done it for us. He has worked out the measure of creativity injected into the economy by any move resulting in reduced unemployment. According to his calculation which has come to be called "Okun's Law", each percentage point reduction in unemployment lifts G.N.P. by 3.2 per cent.[137]

This means that if 15.5 per cent out of 16 per cent unemployment existing in Pakistan in the relevant year was eliminated by the introduction of interest-free banking, the rise in national income would have been of the order of (15.5 x 3.2) 49.60 per cent. We needed a rise of 53.33 per cent in national income, and the introduction of interest-free banking falls short of the target by 3.73 per cent. In quantitative terms, it means that the deficit of Rs. 53.64 billion is contracted to (53.64 ÷ 53.33 x 3.73) Rs. 3.75 billion.

Since the model does not countenance any shortfall in the budgetary balance, it becomes the duty of the model to show how this balance of shortfall can be made up.

We have hitherto considered the impact of interest-free banking on the revenue side of th budget only. It has fairly significant implications on the expenditure side as well. These relate to areas of interest payments on domestic debt, to savings in subsidies, and to de-nationalization of public sector ventures which perpetually run at a loss. We have to see whether these implications are capable of covering the balance of the deficit of Rs. 3.75 billion.

Taking the first item on expenditure side which is directly relevant to the introduction of interest-free banking, we find that the government of Paksitan paid as interest on *domestic* debt a sum of Rs. 15.32 billion in the year 1986-87.[138] This expenditure by definition ceases to exist in an interest-free credit arrangement, as with the maturity of existing securities, all government loans will be shifted over to counter-loan basis. This single item not only washes out the balance of Rs. 3.75 billion of deficit, but converts the budget to a surplus one of the order of (15.32−3.75) Rs. 11.57 billion.

The second item of expenditure on which interest-free banking has an impact, though not an equally direct one, is that of subsidies. In the year under discussion an amount of Rs. 4.84 billion[139] was spent under this head. By and large, this expenditure can be dispensed with, after gainful employment is assured to the lowest strata of the community by interest-free banking. A saving of about Rs. 3 billion appears possible under this head, raising the surplus, after erasing the entire deficit, to Rs. 14.57 billion.

It is difficult to quantify the savings that will occur if all public sector ventures which are running at a loss are turned over to private hands. Budget documents, instead of divulging relevant figures, strive hard, and with substantial success, to conceal them. As an approximation, it would not be an over-estimate that this single step has a potential for saving and generating new income exceeding Rs. 10 billion. Let us have a glimpse of the situation. We know that more than half of the installed productive capacity in the country is in public hands, and except for P.I.A., the banking sector and some relatively minor areas, every public sector venture runs at a loss. Railways, the largest enterprise in the country, runs at a massive loss,[140] although in any private hands the railways would yield almost this much revenue in lease-money and income tax. Identical situation prevails in the matter of Pakistan Steel, the most capital intensive productive enterprise. Karachi Shipyard, ever since its functioning, has always run at a loss. Pakistan Shipping Corporation which, before its nationalization, paid income tax running into tens of millions of rupees, has now to be subsidized by a few hundreds of millions every year. All private oil companies functioning in the country pay tens of millions in taxes and royalties to the government, the only one that has to be subsidized is the one that the government runs itself.

We can shift over every losing venture to private enterprise, and instead of suffering significant losses every year, we can start generating equally significant revenues from these enterprises. In theory, except for doctrinaire socialists, every one agrees. In practice, it cannot be done, notwithstanding repeated government policy announcements in this regard, including the one by the Railways Minister on the floor of the National Assembly on March 14, 1988, that government is willing to hand over even railways to any suitable private party which may be willing to run these.[141] The obstacle is the issue of retrenchment of surplus staff foisted on all public ventures by successive governments for political considerations. No private party will take over any public sector enterprise unless it can fire or retire superfluous staff and functionless employees, and that is what neither the labour unions nor the government, for understandable reasons, can possibly concede.

It is here that interest-free banking comes to have a direct bearing on solving this riddle. As soon as unemployment is eradicated in the country, the political compulsions of both the labour unions and the government cease to exist. Labourers will know that they can get jobs in alternative enterprises, and their reason for hostility against their transfer to private hands will cease to exist. If conditions emerged in which all public enterprises running at a loss could be handed over to private entrepreneurs, who not only earn profit, but also pay income-tax to the government, the total positive impact on the budget of the year under examination may exceed Rs.10 billion.

The cumulative consequence of induction of interest-free banking on the budgetary deficit of the nature and dimensions of the one that relates to the year 1986-87 would be not only to erase the entire deficit of Rs.53.64 billion, but to convert it to a surplus one of approximately Rs.24.57 billion.[142] This incidentally provides opportunity to grasp the meaning of verse 2: 268 of the Quran which in part says, "The Evil one threatens you with poverty and ... God promiseth you His ... bounties ..."

We can therefore conclude that the pre-condition of successful implementation of interest-free banking, in so far as fiscal responsiblity and balanced budget are concerned, is endogenously within its competence. This competence ensures that the new system, far from generating any inflationary pressure by its productive expansionism, will be able to call a halt to inflationary pressures that already exist on account of consumptional expansionism, which has blighted almost every economy in the free world for the last several decades.

Monetary Management Mechanism

We can now proceed to the ninth obstacle in the path of interest-free banking and decide for ourselves whether the model has any in-built capability of traversing it. Under point (4) relating to producing equilibrium between demand and supply of loans at zero rate of interest, we overthrew statutory reserve of banks and created the required equiliblium. This means that with the adoption of this model, two significant monetary management instruments viz., interest and bank reserve cease to exist. Unless some alternative mechanism is devised, the monetary authority will have, except for open market operations, no instrument left to control the magnitude of credit.

As Keynes puts it "with the disappearance of ... rentier aspect much else .. besides will suffer a sea-change."[143] An analogy from the sea might help clear the situation. When we shifted from sails and oars to the marine engine, the ships started sailing the seas without the help of sails and oars. With the introduction of interest-free banking, we do not need the sails and oars of bank rate and statutory reserve.

We needed these instruments because we had not been able to devise the marine engine of interest-free banking for the ships of our economy. If we succeed in devising this engine which ensures co-existence of growth and stability, monetary management instruments become by and large redundant.

In fact, if we look at the issue closely, these have already become substantially obsolete. Let us first take the bank rate. It is supposed to be a major instrument in the hands of the monetary authorities, whose lowering and raising can be used as effective weapons to expand and contract economy, to fight against unemployment and inflation respectively. But when we are confronted with both unemployment and inflation, as the entire free world has been since 1965, the bank rate policy ceases to remain meaningful. True, main industrial countries still continue to use the bank rate when either of the two maladies appears more threatening but the act simultaneously aggravates the situation in the opposite direction. This means that bank rate as an instrument of monetary policy has already lost the potency that books on economics continue to assign to it.

In contrast to this situation the model under examination has a built-in arrangement to help any economy to outgrow both unemployment and inflation. Elimination of interest assures employment to all. Elimination of consumptional expansionism, concepts of counter-loan, 110 per cent collateral,and above all rigorous selective credit control including fiscal balance exclude all chances of inflation. In the absence of both unemployment and inflation the very need to artificially expand or contract the economy ceases to exist.

Let us look at the role of statutory reserve as an instrument of monetary management. In early nineteen-twenties of this century, proposals appear to have been first made to utilize reserve ratio in order to control the credit base of commercial banks. It was in 1933 that official recognition was first given to this aspect of bank reserve "in the United States in the Thomas Amendment to the Agricultural Adjustment Act."[144] Since then, it has not often been used as an instrument of monetary management. So far as the developing countries are concerned, some central banks do not have the authority to vary reserve requirments, e.g., India, and there are others who in spite of the possession of this authority have not used it, e.g., Pakistan.

Yet the elimination of interest and statutory reserve in the TMCL banking model, does not make it incapable of devising new instruments of credit control. In the main it is the counter-loan ratio which emerges as the alternative to bank-rate policy. Just as monetary authority changes bank rate in order either to stimulate or restrain an economy, in the new model it can achieve identical results by lowering or raising the counter-loan ratio respectively. Productive expansionism is so deeply ingrained in the model that lowering counter-loan may perhaps never be needed. Raising the ratio can conceivably be needed in periods of particular stress like those of war or during some period after the war.

Similar is the position of the collateral whose measure can be raised from 110 per cent suggested in the model to 120 or 130 per cent or even higher, but cannot be lowered to less than 100 per cent. This is because the model itself is unlikely to need any further injection of expansionism, though restraining could conceivably become necessary under extraordinary circumstances for which a large elbow room exists in the model.

To sum up with the installation of the marine engine, although sails and oars will become redundant, if a mechanical defect occurs in the engine, it is capable of putting forth alternative propelling mechanism, without needing recourse to sails and oars. Thus it is that the intrest-free banking is capable of crossing the ninth hurdle in its way relating to mechanism of credit control.

Profitability of TMCL Banks

We now reach the tenth and last obstacle in the path of interest-free banking. If these banks will neither pay any interest on deposits nor receive any interest, these will presumably have no income. *Prima facie,* these will not be able to pay their way, much less make a worthwhile profit which limits the workability of the model to nationalized banks, whose expenses can be met by an annual subsidy from the government. As these banks will not be motivated by profit, their efficiency and competence in management will fall even lower than what obtains in nationalized banks of Pakistan. Fortunately, we are not forced to make that unhappy choice as the model, contrary to what appears on the surface, is pregnant with possibilities of profit exceeding even those that present pattern of banking can yield. The secret of this enhanced level of profitability lies primarily in the extinction of bank reserve, and secondarily in the vast enhancement in the quantum of loans, and as a necessary consequence the vast inflow of counter-loans which, even after providing for liquidity, leaves such massive amounts with the banking system that its direct productive investment, even at such a low rate of profit as 10 per cent, enables the counter loan model to earn profit far exceeding the one available to conventional banks.

We have already seen that every advance will be matched by 12-1/2 per cent of counter-loan for 8 multiples of time of loan availability. We have already drawn 4-1/2 percentage points of these counter-loans by keeping 2 percentage points in the till, and advancing 2-1/2 percentage points to the central bank to generate a total liquidity of 22 per cent of all deposits.

What is the bank to do with the balance of 8 percentage points of counter-loans? For this part of its resources, the bank will assume the role of an investment bank in the most direct sense. The obvious openings are the stock exchange, real estate, and Participation Term Certificates in existing industries.[146] These, however, are likely to prove inadequate openings for the vast amounts of constantly increasing funds which this basis of lending is likely to cast in the coffers of these banks. They will, therefore, have to institute holding companies which will invest directly, consistent with national priorities and objectives, in such industrial and commercial ventures which are likely to give the highest return. Capital intensive ventures are likely to prove more in consonance with the resources available to these banks.

A simulated exercise was undertaken to compare the income likely to be available under TMCL banking with the one available to traditional banks in Pakistan. The parameters determining the income of traditional banks were the ones existing in the country at the time of calculation (1985). These were turn-over period of bank advances as forty days,[147] statutory reserve 35%, inclusive of 25% invested in treasury bills and earning 6% interest; weighted average of interest paid on deposits 5.95% and the one received on advances 11.20 per cent. Under both varieties of banking, the total deposits were assumed to be, for the sake of simplicity, Rs. 1,000, rising at the rate of 39.53 per cent per year which was the average for the last ten years.

The turn-over period in the case of TMCL banking was assumed to stay at 40 days, neglecting the likely increase in velocity, to facilitate comparison of income. Of course, in the case of this banking there is neither any traditional reserve nor any interest is paid on deposits or claimed on advances. Eight percentage points of counter-loans are directly invested, and are assumed to earn an average return of 10% per year on the investment.

The result of this simulated exercise spread over six extensive tables each needing to be folded twice or thrice, to conform to the format of this book, cannot be included here.[148] However, these have been checked and rechecked by several competent and responsible banking and audit authorities at the highest available level in the country. The end result of these six tables in a tabloid form is presented below, on the assumptions already spelled out.

Comparative Gross Income of Traditional & TMCL Banks

(Total Deposits of Each Banking System Rs. 1000)

Year of Working	Income of Traditional Banks	Income of TMCL Banks	Income of TMCL Banks as Percentage of income of Traditional Banks
Ist year	Rs. 64.48	Rs. 39.96	61.97 per cent
2nd Year	Rs. 172.43	Rs. 242.36	140.55 per cent
3rd year .	Rs. 484.06	Rs. 1317.86	272.25 per cent

This table indicates that while TMCL banks earn less than two-third of the income of traditional banks in the first year, the income of the former is slightly short of three multiples of the income of the latter in the third year. It appears from examination of detailed tables, and is even reflected in the tabloid table given above that while income of traditional banks rises in some kind of arithmetical progression, the rise in income of TMCL banks is fairly close to geometrical progression.

Objective reality is often more eloquent than any argument. The result of this simulated exercise indicates that no apprehension need be entertained regarding the income potential of banking under TMCL arrangement. This concept, far from requiring some kind of subsidy for its working, is incomparably far more profitable than the current system. The only difference is that this vast enhancement of income of the banking sector emerges on account of the prosperity of the people, and not through their exploitation and impoverishment.

Interest-free banking is therefore fully capable of crossing over the tenth and last conceptual hurdle placed in its way.

First Tentative Word Though Not the Last

Having successfully met all the ten pre-conditions for the evolution of an interest-free banking model, the TMCL concept can be regarded the only viable, workable and feasible substitute for interest. All other concepts of which we are aware cannot cross even the first hurdle of providing a mechanism for encashment of a premature commercial paper at face value without resorting to one or another variety of subterfuge for discounting. TMCL concept alone enables us to purchase any quantity of commercial papers at face value without feeling any variety of deprivation. If no other concept available so far shows any remote capability of crossing even the first hurdle and TMCL concept indicates competence of crossing all the ten, it is a significant achievement in the history of man's struggle to secure release from the depredation of interest, of which evidence extends to 4000 years. It also brings first positive result to the long struggle of Judaic, Christian, and Muslim scholars to discover a workable substitute for interest.

This, however, cannot be regarded as the last word. Not by a long stretch. More competent men in the days to come will almost certainly improve and amplify it, and even possibly produce a better alternative. In particular, the crucible of experience is bound to burnish it far beyond its present shape. But for a long time perhaps, it may be deemed the first break-through in the long struggle of man to liberate himself from the depredation of interest.

CHAPTER – III
Modalities of Change Over

The Question of Strategy

Having crossed over the basic hurdles, we can proceed to the question of strategy so that the transition is smooth and avoids possible distortions. It is from this point of view that the principle of gradualism will need to be adopted. How fast or how slow this gradualism should be are difficult questions to answer. No hard and fast rule can be prescribed. Every country which accepts the basic principles of interest-free banking will have to decide its pace in the context of its economy and its environment.

The suggestion that is being made is in the context of Pakistan. With slight variations in the matter of pace, it will apply to most Third World countries. The pace will need to be significantly lowered in the case of developed countries, but the strategy in all cases will be identical.

The strategy is to lower in a number of steps, the interest rate, the reserve ratio and the fiscal deficit by an identical percentage. Some belt-tightening will be involved initially by this last measure till the productive expansionism of the first two items is reflected in government receipts. But even the difficulty of initiation can be kept within managable proportions by plugging leakages of collection and checking wasteful expenditure, and for the balance imposing an across-the-board cut on non-developmental expenditure. Some steps which do not involve inordinate political reprecussions, like selling out some of the white elephants like O.G.D.C. and National Shipping Corporation would lend some helping hand.

In the context of Pakistan, the shift over is suggested to be spread over a period of about ten years with five more or less equivalent steps in the direction of reducing the three magnitudes of interest-rate, reserve ratio, and fiscal deficit to zero. This is dictated by the consideration that significant results will not be obtained if less than 20% reduction is effected in the three directions, as a first step, and possibly even subsequent steps.

The First Three Rounds of Steps

Specifically speaking, the first round of steps may comprise lowering the bank rate from 10% to 8%, the spread, *i.e.*, the difference between the bank rate and the lending rate, which is grossly inflated anyway, from 8% to 6%, so that the lending rate falls from the present 18% to 14%, which obtained before we "abolished interest". Simultaneously, the reserve ratio should be lowered to about 28 per cent to increase credit capability of banks commensurate with increased demand of loans, besides 20% trimming of fiscal deficit. We should then watch the reaction of the economy in the matter of pace of growth.

If before taking the steps indicated, the economy was growing at the annual pace of 6% and, after somewhere around two years, it starts growing by nearly 7%, time will have come to take the next round of steps of identical reductions in the three directions. Belt-tightening in the matter of budget control will appear less severe this time because enhanced pace of growth will start reflecting itself in government receipts. Yet some belt-tightening has to stay as the second move towards further lowering of bank rate to 6%, lending rate from 14% to 10% and of reserve ratio to perhaps 22%, must be accompanied by further narrowing of the deficit by at least 20%,[149] which may have to be made manageable by various actions suggested in this relation in the context of the first step, besides reduction of such subsidies as may be possible, and selling some more loss-incurring public sector ventures.

Having allowed about two years to watch the result of our second round of steps of lowering the three magnitudes, we should look to the signal of the pace of growth. If it has touched or exceeded 8%, we should proceed to the third step of lowering the bank rate to 4%, the lending rate to 7% and the reserve ratio to 18%. Again, at this stage, the magnitude of government deficit should also simultaneously fall by another 20% which may perhaps be somewhat easier on account of the enhanced revenues reflecting the consistent rise in the growth rate. Denationalization and deregulationization should be actively pursued all the while, so that increased production and increased efficiency of productive process including activation of sick mills, can sop up consistent increase in credit. Unproductive lending should be reduced to the trickle necessary to meet the residue of fiscal deficit.

Mid-Operation Review

Immediately after introducing the third round of reductions already indicated, an in-depth appraisal of the functioning of the economy should be taken in hand. The ever increasing tempo of growth can create some problems which can be beyond the competence of the market to attend to, largely because these fall in the jurisdiction of the government.

What can be foreseen, at this distance in time and in this highly conjectural context, is that there may be significant pressure on nationalized banking and infrastructural facilities, including in particular energy and communications. With consistent constraints on the budget which is a built-in part of the model, notwithstanding continuous rise in revenue, the government is unlikely to provide major improvements calling for large chunks of investment. In such a situation when caution falters, courage and vision become more worthy of reliance. By the time of mid term of change over, if not earlier, government should seriously explore handing over of banking, railways, telephones, and even production and distribution of electric energy to private enterprise.

Denationalization of Banking

By the time we start on the third round of steps for

change over to interest-free economy, we should have already denationalized our banks. The consistent fall in the quality of managerial competence ever since their nationalization makes them distinctly unqualified to take over the enormous expansion of credit that the model entails. If this expansion tends to compound sloth, indifference and incompetence, as is likely, on account of the bureaucratic posture adopted by many bankers, and most of subordinate staff, it can injure the purposes and objectives of opting for interest-free banking. Only one facet of the incompetence is enough to clinch the decision. Compare the magnitude of embezzelments and hold-up cases in nationalized banks with their virtual non-existence in private banking sector, although manned by Pakistanis of identical background and training. Even the limited managerial competence of banking in the nationalized sector is further diluted by the myopic interference of political and bureaucratic superiors which include demands for inordinate relaxations in normal banking practices in particular cases. Again, only one example will be enough. There are innumerable cases of loans having been advanced without collateral under political pressure, their subsequent writing off under indentical pressure, coupled with the audacity to decline to give names of such beneficiaries even to the Federal Public Accounts Committee which obviously cannot be done without political cover. When the issue was raised on the floor of the National Assembly, the government declined to divulge the names. This alone is enough to show the absolute necessity of releasing banking from political bribery under the guise of nationalization.

Denationalization of Transport and Communication Sector

Even without the induction of the model, with its pressures of growth, railways are diseased to the core. Its first class is a long way inferior to the second class of pre-partition days; food available during journeys is atrocious; bribery is rampant at virtually every level; the railway stations are so filthy that on occasion, one can mistake them for filth depots.

On the top of it, government is under pressure to provide billions for development every year, besides footing the bill of the deficit of running them which was 1.6 billion in 1986-87. The foolish view that the government is bearing all this burden in the interest of the poor travellers falls apart on slightest reflection. Private enterprise cannot afford to raise fares beyond the reach of these very poor travellers. Otherwise, it will lose clientele to road transport. Market knows how to determine these things and also knows how to communicate its message. Efficient functioning cannot be delinked from the profit motive as even socialist countries have started learning. Let us shift over from this haemorrhage of scarce resources, to some annual lease money and to some income tax when private enterprise imparts profitability into the system, a variety of alchemy of which private enterprise alone has the monoply.

This point is proved by the experience of Japan. The Japanese National Railways, till 1987, were losing about $ 14 billion a year. Total debts, incurred by the railways had mounted to a staggering $ 281 billion, a sum equal to combined debt of Argentina, Brazil and Mexico. Within twelve months of denationalization, each of the seven new companies which had taken over regional chunks of this major complex, produced a modest profit, cumulatively reaching the level of pre-tax profit of 1.2 billion dollars.[149-A]

The same is the situation in relation to electricity and telephones. The details are known to every one and a short book will not bear their narration. More than 25 per cent loss in distribution of electricity, admitted by the government, is such a stupendous one that this alone will justify handing over distribution to private enterprise. Far deeper maladies run through the entire telephone system, leaving no chance for any remedy except the drastic one of handing it over to private enterprise. The income that telephone service yields at present will prove a long way short of lease money and income tax that this service is likely to pay, if handed over to private sector, apart from accelerated pace of expansion and exceptional enhancement of efficiency.

Activation of Energy Sector

In the energy sector, we have been exceptionally out of step with the demands of the situation, otherwise we should have been self-sufficient in oil by now. For more than two decades, we insisted on sticking to policies of squeezing to the ultimate limit the two foreign oil companies whose only fault was that they had discovered gas and oil in the country. This not only called a halt to further exploration of energy sites by these two companies but shied away other foreign companies from entering the field. We insisted on banking on OGDC to find the needed oil. When it failed signally to deliver the goods, as could have been anticipated, relaxations of policy in the right direction were introduced, with the result that from declining oil production we shifted to increasing oil production. Whatever further relaxation will maximise production in this area, without involving scarce government resources, should be made anyway, but should positively be made by the time of starting on the shift over from interest-oriented economy to interest-free economy. This will go a long way in meeting increasing requirements of energy in an expanding economy, bring in sizeable revenues to government exchequer, besides narrowing the yawning gap in our foreign trade deficit.

The Price-Line

Our mid-term review should particularly focus attention on the price-line. Although *general* inflation is unlikely to occur if consistent reduction in fiscal deficit and other policies already indicated are adhered to, pressure can emerge in areas where supplies fail to keep pace with likely increase in demand, reflecting increased prosperity. In the consumptional sector, things like meat, milk, sugar, vegetable oil are likely to exhibit this tendency which should be countered by appropriate policies ensuring their increased production. It should be recognized that though fruitful short-term measures can be adopted, a review of agricultural policies in general, and land tenure policies in particular, has to be taken in hand to generate the necessary equilibrium.

It should be ensured that we have arranged to provide for a significant increase in the tempo of building construction activities. Though market can be depended upon to cater to these needs, it may be helpful if the policy-maker ensures the erection of additional plants for cement, mechanical brick production, and other necessary building requirements.

In the unlikely event of any pressure becoming visible on the general price-line, reducing budgetary deficit will come to assume a higher priority, compared with the other two parameters of the model, *viz.*,lowering interest and lowering statutory reserve. The methodology of contracting deficit has already been indicated earlier, and details can only be worked out at a given time and space.

If, as a theoretical consideration, there is a perceptible pressure on the price-line at the fourth or fifth stage of downward revision of the three instruments of the model, we will need to lower the pace of shift over, and prematurely introduce the concept of counter-loan, although at about a quarter of its proposed level at the fourth stage and a half of it at the fifth. Under no circumstances should there be any relapse in the direction of either raising the rate or raising the statutory reserve. These observations are being made by way of abundant caution, and not because of any likelihood of emergence of any situation which may call for these remedial measures.

Taxation Policy

We have hitherto not said a word about raising taxes to meet the target of extinction of budgetary deficit. This is because it is at variance with the growth strategy of the model, on which primary reliance has been placed to boost governmental receipts. All the same, the basic purpose is more important than the strategy adopted. If productive expansionism does not give all the help that the model calls for in the direction of extinction of fiscal deficit, slight increase in taxation may be resorted to.

Labour Policy

Our mid-operation review is likely to show that although unemployment survives at least at half the level it existed before we started working on the model, shortages of various skilled varieties have already emerged. Vast expansion in training programmes and imparting of technical skills should be taken in hand right at the start of the change over, and its deepening and widening should be undertaken with renewed zest at every stage of the operation. Private enterprise may be asked to lend a helping hand and tax deductions should be allowed for whatever is done in this direction.

Land Reforms

While productive expansionism which is the goal of the model will start exhibiting significant results in the industrial and commercial sectors, agriculture may continue to look like a laggard. As the bulk of the population is dependent on agriculture, prosperity will not reach the people who most deserve it and need to receive its benefits.

Agriculture is not merely starved for credit, for which the model provides the requisite remedy. It is structurally incapable of galvanizing itself to the level of productive expansionism the model calls for. The obvious hindrances are an archaic land tenure system and an absolutely unworkable fragmentation of holdings.

In the matter of land tenure, with every move in the direction of extinction of interest, other varieties of unearned income will start coming under the focus of deepening disapproval. It should not be forgotten that the Holy Prophet regarded both share-cropping and rent as interest. There are several *ahadith* reported in both *Bukhari,* and *Muslim* besides *Tirmadhi, Abu Daud, Ibn Majah* and *Nasa'i* in which the Holy Prophet has prohibited both share-cropping and rent of land. According to a *hadith* reported by Jabir Bin Abdullah in *Abu Daud,* the Holy Prophet has used the words of "take notice of war from Allah and His Apostle"[150] while prohibiting *mukhabara* which means share-cropping. This is the very construction which the Quran has used for prohibition of interest. If share-cropping is that close to interest, renting out land is obviously closer to it. Once Muslims succeed in evolving an interest-free banking structure, other forms of unearned income will start looking suspect in their eyes.

Approval accorded at present to both share-cropping and rent of land is a part of the long monarchical-feudal history through which the *ummah* has lived hitherto. Acceptance of the social philosophy of Islam and in particular of its abhorrence of interest will increasingly persuade Muslims to disapprove the institution of the absentee landlord.

In pristine Islam, except for the paramountcy of social considerations, there is no upper limit to holdings which are self-cultivated, just as there is no lower limit to the ones which are not. But political power of the landlord who has hitherto dominated most of our legislatures stands in the way. So, let us go by stages even here. Holdings of absentee landlords should be reduced by at least 50% compared to the maximum limit permissible at present.

But a hindrance of even greater magnitude is the fragmentation of holdings. Some holdings are very small, and yet these are not in one place. Obviously, no philosophy of social prosperity can fructify in the face of these fragmented holdings. These have to be unified if productivity in agriculture is desired to grow at a pace consistent with other sectors of the economy. In the context of Pakistan, it may be regarded as an essential ingredient of the methodology of shift-over from interest-oriented banking to interest-free banking.

At the start of the shift over, it should be accepted as a principle of policy, that all land-holders whether large, medium or small, should consolidate their holdings in one place. They should be given a five year period to do so on a voluntary basis. Whether they sell and buy or exchange plots with holders placed in an identical position is their business. After five years, compulsory consolidation operation should be initiated so as to be completed by the D-day, the day on which interest is reduced to zero. What measure of compulsion is necessary depends upon circumstances of a given situation.

So far as absentee landlordism is concerned, it cannot long survive the abolition of interest.

Public Involvement in the Programme

The process of shift over to interest-free banking makes such significant departures from current academic thought, whether capitalistic or socialistic, that its acceptance at the policy-making level will not prove adequate. The model and its strategies should pass through the mill of wide-ranging public debate, until political and intellectual elite are persuaded by the enthusiastic zeal of the masses to reach the goals spelled out both by *shari'ah* and the founding fathers of this country.

It is the intellectual elite who through their creative criticism, generate a climate in which political parties can take over the ball and carry it to the goal of national purpose. The decision of the policy maker is of course important, but the idea should be pushed from below instead of being imposed from above. It is time that men of goodwill, spearheaded by thinkers and writers, come forward to give a habitation and a home to the social purposes of the Pakistan Movement.

Let us decide whether or not in the inimitable language of the Holy Quran *rizkun kareem i.e.* "provision honourable" is the goal of social policy in Islam. Time has now come for us to spell out the meaning that we can give to the observation of Iqbal, in his famous Allahabad address, "The nature of the Holy Prophet's religious experience ... is ... creative of a social order."[151] We need to give some time to ponder over the question posed by Iqbal, in his letters to Jinnah, "How is it possible to solve the problem of Muslim poverty?" [152] We also need to amplify the meaning of the answer given by him, "Happily there is a solution in the enforcement of the Law of Islam and its further development in the light of modern ideas..."[153] as also that of the caveat, "if this system of Law is properly understood and applied."[154] We owe it to ourselves to enunciate the meaning of the observation of Iqbal to the effect: "For Islam the acceptance of social democracy in some suitable form is not a revolution, but a return to the original purity of Islam."[155]

Social democracy obviously means political democracy plus economic democracy. While we have been remiss in the former, we have been virtually indifferent to the latter. The model that has been presented primarily concerns itself with economic democracy, but takes leave to plead for its acceptance in the context of political democracy.

Even political democracy needs to mean much more than it has meant for us hitherto. It does not merely mean fair elections, after regular intervals, for Federal and Provincial Assemblies. It also means decentralization of governmental functions from these levels to divisional, district, *tehsil,* and sub-*tehsil* levels. People, through the elective principle, should be allowed to govern themselves right from the grass-root levels of a village and a *mohalla,* endowed with powers and resource-generating competence to attend to settlement of small disputes, law and order, primary education, elementary medical facilities, sanitation and, above all, productive employment of local resources and manpower.

Zakat

It is at this level, and at this level alone, that we can revert to the Quranic version of *zakat*, which does not accept any difference in meaning between *sadaqah* and *zakat.* It is only at the grass-roots level where the elected representatives of the people can know who are the unendowed old and the sick, the widows and the orphans, who are the bright children who cannot study for want of support, who are the unemployed young men who need to be employed, and set up suitable productive units for them through such expertise and resources as they can raise locally, supplemented by such credit as may be necessary, and can be made available by the new interest-free credit system.

Elected representatives of the people at grass-root levels come to have an incomparable awareness regarding the magnitude of resources necessary to meet their requirements, and, also, who are the people who can afford to provide help to their under-endowed neighbours. It is this awareness which under the watchful eyes of the citizens can ensure proper collection and disbursement of *zakat*. It is not the business, in the modern context, of any federal or provincial government to do it, as the movement of collection first to the coffers of the government and its later flow back for disbursement around the points of collection needlessly involves two movements, pregnant with possibilities of leakage in themselves, but even more, the mere act of delinking of collection and disbursement deprives the one who pays of the essential knowledge of how it has been spent. When a major portion of *zakat* disbursement becomes an instrument for political patronage under the auspices of the government, and this is supplemented by leakages and downright embezzlements, these clog the springs of social concern. We must hasten to re-activate these springs by entrusting both collection and disbursement of zakat to democratically elected grass-root level local governments.

Corruption

No social philosophy can be meaningfully implemented in a corrupt environment. The introduction of the monetary model of interest-free banking can make a contribution in the direction of excluding the necessity of making wrongful gains by eliminating privation. But we find corruption even more prevalent among sections of society which are blessed with affluence. These are the cause of major concern. It is precisely here that the model does not indicate any competence to provide the answer.

The deterrence that is necessary has got to come from a re-examination and reshaping of the relevant official regulations and the law of the land. Even a superficial examination is enough to indicate that these not only fail to meet the magnitude of the situation, but appear to spread the disease to an ever-widening circle. Once a corrupt official knows that the maximum civil punishment that can be given to him is removal from his office, it ceases to be a deterrent to any one who has already amassed sufficient fortune to derive lucrative benefit from its investment. Those who have not reached that position strive hard to attain it. In such a situation, it is difficult to decide whether the punishment is more of an inducement or a deterrent.

Similar is the position of criminal law. Maximum punishment provided by law is two years rigorous imprisonment. If a person has collected a couple of millions by corrupt practices, he tends to view with equanimity the risk of going to jail, if at all it comes to that. The cost appears well worth the prize. He would be glad to go to jail for another two years, if another two millions were given to him.

It is obvious that neither the civil nor the criminal punishment nor both of them put together are tailored to fit the nature of the offence. Unless confiscation of property and other assets forms an integral part of the punishment, the malady will not be cured. The fear of losing everything will force every one to think twice before indulging in corruption.

Foreign Policy

During the period of shift-over from interest-oriented to interest-free economy, it would be helpful to wear a low profile in foreign policy. While we should deepen our friendship with our friends, we should perservere in striving for improvement in relations on a reciprocal basis with those who are not. Revolutionary changes that would be taking place in the economy will demand all our energy and all our attention. We cannot afford to give anything less to them. We will be on a historic voyage towards a new and glorious destiny and we cannot afford any extrinsic factors to deviate us from our destination.

Resumption of Shift-Over Operation

Having completed the third stage of our shift-over, besides meeting the demands that a mid-term review may pose for us, we should again look at our barometer, *viz.*, the growth rate. If eight per cent growth rate was the level from which we started our third stage, and this has improved its pace to nine per cent during a two year period or thereabout, time has come to proceed to the fourth stage, in which loan rate should fall to somewhat between three and four per cent, the bank rate between one and half to two per cent, the reserve ratio to 15% and the fiscal deficit should shrink by another 20%. The residue of fiscal deficit should preferably not exceed 0.5 per cent of G.N.P. at the end of the fourth stage. If this is not achieved in the first year of the operation of the fourth stage, it should be achieved by the second year on account of enhanced revenue generation potential of this stage, accompanied as it is by the policy thrusts in the laggard sectors indicated by our mid-third-stage review. Some time during the third or the fourth stage, at the latest, consideration should be given to deposit insurance. This is already in operation in U.S.A. Details can be amended to suit the context of this country.

As we reach the fifth and the final stage, we shall look at two barometers, *viz.*, growth rate which should rise another one per cent to 10 per cent, and fiscal deficit should not exceed 0.5 per cent of G.N.P. If these indicators or something thereabout has been attained, we can fix a suitable D-day from which fiscal deficit, interest rate and statutory reserve will be reduced to zero, and the entire economy will shift over to interest-free banking. From the D-day, the entire model already spelled out in Chapter II will become operative. If we started the operation of shift-over from interest-oriented to interest-free economy at a growth rate of 6 per cent, as has been assumed in expounding the modalities of the shift-over operation, after the D-day the economy of the country will reach and continue growing at a steady pace of *at least* 12 per cent.

It may be pointed out that the rate of growth resulting from shift over to interest free economy has advisedly been denoted at an extremely conservative level. It is likely to be much higher than has been indicated, when we keep in view the fact that South Korea, employing in the main the strategy of free enterprise, succeeded in multiplying its G.N.P. 18 times in 21 years. There is no reason for us, when we join extinction of exploitation with free enterprise, not to do equally well. The probability of growth rate is likely to be 18% or thereabout rather than 12% that has been indicated. But even if G.N.P. of Pakistan grew at the lower estimate, it will exceed that of India in the 23rd year after the introduction of interest-free banking, after allowing for growth of Indian economy as its average of 3.7% for the last two decades. But if the pace of growth reaches 18% in Pakistan, which is by no means unlikely, the G.N.P. of Pakistan will overtake that of India in the 14th year, after allowing for the indicated Indian growth. However, much depends on the level of understanding, vision, enthusiasm, and competent management which is brought to bear on the execution of the model. But whatever time it takes for the Pakistan economy to outgrow Indian economy, the ideology of Pakistan will have been vindicated.

It must however be emphasized that while the instruments indicated in the model, *viz.*, zero rates of interest, statutory reserve and fiscal deficit are absolute and unalterable, whichever country adopts the model, the various percentages and targets mentioned under modalities of shift over are indicative and not absolute. While these will by necessity undergo a change in the context of every other country, even in Pakistan, these may not turn out to be as tailor-made as appears to be indicated by the modalities of shift-over. They are provisional and illustrative, though the movement of the economy and its pace is likely to be in the direction indicated. Even the two-year period, suggested for every stage, would be subject to revision at every stage. A vigilant monitoring authority will consistently prod planning policy to provide guidance in the matter of detail.

Government Securities

During the course of the shift-over, the government will continue securing loans, on the basis of interest, reflecting the consistently reduced rate of interest at every stage. On the D-day, there will be a magnitude of rupee-debt represented by these interest-earning securities which the government may not like to shift over to counter-loan basis, on account of the magnitude of counter-loan involved, besides possible legal constraints to unilateral annulment of interest on these securities. These securities will therefore continue paying interest till their maturity.

After D-day, no securities will be sold by the government except on counter-loan basis. Assuming 12-1/2% be the level of counter-loan fixed by the monetary authority, government will have to pay one eighth of the amount it intends to raise by the sale of any issue of securities. This counter-loan will be advanced for 8 multiples of the period of time involved in the maturity of these securities. Whichever interest-bearing government paper matures after D-day, it will have the option of refund or conversion to a new counter-loan based security. Their subsequent sale and purchase in the money market will also be on the same basis.

It may be asked as to why should government borrow at all after the D-day, when it has ceased to run any deficit, and why should banks lend to it when new securities do not earn any interest. Government can have productive projects in hand for which it can need to borrow money, and it would be entirely consistent with the model for banks to lend money to the government for productive purposes. As to why they should do so, even though the securities earn no interest, the reply is for the same reason for which they lend money without interest to every one else, *viz.*, making a profit on the investment of the greater part of the counter-loan.

Foreign Debt

In this interest-oriented world, if a country chooses to shift to interest-free economy, it needs to be considered as to what will happen to its foreign debts. Naturally, no country has the power to impose its social philosophy on any other country, much less the whole wide world. Therefore, interest on foreign debts which will stand payable on the D-day will have to be paid even after D-day.

Interest-free banking does not claim competence to solve all economic problems of any country that chooses to adopt it, and foreign debts by definition fall outside its jurisdiction. However, since it does claim to solve the two most intractable problems that blight most economies in the so-called free world, *viz.*, unemployment and inflation, and as a necessary consequence claims capability of conferring accelerated pace of growth undisturbed by instability, it cannot fail to have a positive impact on foreign trade and therefore on balance of payments. Accelerated growth, and a consistent one at that, is bound to generate export potential on the one side and to expand the area of import substitution on the other, narrowing the negative gap between the two, until it ceases to exist, and therefore extinguishing the necessity of contracting further foreign loans. In due course, it is likely to generate the capability of even starting repaying these.

It is not possible to determine the period, at this distance of time and in such a hypothetical context, before this healthy development in the area of foreign trade, enables us to meet the magnitude of servicing the foreign debts which will already have been contracted before our adverse trade gap is narrowed to zero. This period can be long, and until we decide on shift-over and even during initial stages of shift-over to interest-free economy, things can become worse before these become better. But the basic point is that unless we adopt this principle of accelerated growth, we may find our economy drowning ever deeper into the morass of foreign debt. Therefore, although interest-free economy does not have any direct bearing on extinction of foreign interest-bearing debts, it is the only strategy which indirectly enables us to meet this inordinate burden, and eventually even makes us capable of winning release from it.

For the present, the situation is that during the latest year (1986-87) for which figures are available, we ran a deficit of $ 2.28 billion, as we imported goods worth $5.78 billion and exported goods worth $3.49 billion. However, this adverse balance was more than wiped out by private unrequited transfers (mainly remittances of Pakistanis working in foreign countries) amounting to $2.50 billion, though services sector reintroduces a negative magnitude of $0.97 billion.[156]

This means that we may not have been forced to seek foreign assistance to the tune of $1.59 billion in 1986-87, if we did not have to pay $1.22 billion to service our accumulated previous debt of $11.7 billion as on 31st December 1986.[157] This shows that 76.85 per cent of the foreign loans (euphemistically called aid) raised in this year was never received by us, but was deducted at source to pay primarily interest on loans already borrowed. We received only 23.15 cents for every dollar for which we wrote our IOU.

Things could have been much worse if we did not receive $ 2.5 billion from our compatriots working abroad. Pressures could mount beyond the endurance of our economy. Since these remittances are unlikely to continue for long, we have to look around for some strategy of accelerated growth to meet the basic difference of the ratio of one to two between our exports and imports. So far as this writer is aware, no strategy better than introduction of interest-free banking can come to our rescue.

CHAPTER – IV
Answers To Possible Objections

Every innovative idea has the responsibiltiy of visualizing objections that can be raised against it and attempt to meet them in advance. This can help provide a meanigful direction to a debate which can possibly ensue. As this one is likely to be under attack not only from the right and the left, but even from some fundamentalists of Islamism, it may perhaps be fair to give answers to questions which appear likely to be raised.

Answers to Capitalistic Critics

The model presented roots out the very foundation stone of capitalism, and must attract its antagonism and wrath. There is nothing that can be done to avoid it, except to appeal to rationality to which every camp including capitalism lays claim, to get beyond its myths and mythologies like its theories of interest, its notion of interest as a rationing device, its saving mobilization potential, a necessary opportunity cost, a payment for scarcity of capital, even though self-created, a payment for loss of value in an inflationary context, even though self-created again, so that we can proceed from the unending game of beating about the bush to the basic problems that toiling masses around the globe suffer from *viz.*, privation, indignity, unemployment and inflation. Since these are the direct consequences of the institution of interest, no matter whether it is the corner-stone of the capitalistic superstructure, it has to be under attack, and it is for capitalistic economics to decide whether it will prefer to accept what rationality dictates, or continue expending all its extraordinary intellectual talent in churning chicanery to push all unanswerable issues under the rug of myths and mythologies already mentioned. We shall not repeat the reasons already given though, somewhat too briefly, in Chapter I as to why these notions deserve these epithets.

If capitalistic economics may be willing to stick to what it has been projecting as its ultimate purpose, *viz.*, human welfare, sophistry apart, it will not be able to sustain any of these theories and postures. There are two levels at which these can be disproved or at least create the necessity of re-examination. One is examination in depth of every argument that has hitherto been advanced to sustain this exploitative institution. This short book will not permit this exercise which in the nature of things calls for an exposition extending to almost a thousand pages. So much has been written in favour of interest that even selective repudiation, however concisely undertaken, cannot take much less than that much space. This has been attempted in *Man and Money,* which is in final stages of revision before publication. The present book, primarily concerned as it is with the exposition of an interest-free banking model and the modalities of its introduction, has had to content itself to compressing to a couple of paragraphs or so, the repudiation of the more significant props raised in support of this exploitative institution. Only theories of interest which have already been unanswerably repudiated by Bohm Bawerk have been skipped over to save space.

The same is the position in respect of another fundamental posture adopted by the model on which its acceptability or otherwise in the ultimate analysis may come to depend. If social welfare is the ultimate goal of economics, it cannot countenance either unemployment or inflation, much less their combined infliction of misery on man. What answer does economics possess, within its parameters of acceptance of both interest and statutory reserve, which may enable man to liberate himself from both the scourges of unemployment and inflation *simultaneously,* without pushing him into the arms of one or the other version of a totalitarian state?

If efforts of some of the keenest minds extending to over three hundred years have not yet been able to evolve a single persuasive reason for the validity of interest, and if as its inescapable consequence, ineradicable unemployment and inflation must persist, and if privations engendered by these and several other consequences of interest are no longer acceptable to vast masses of mankind, men gifted with social concern have no option left except to re-examine the related issues and, if necessary, to repudiate the entire posture of economics in relation to interest, lock, stock and barrel. When we reach that far, we will need to have a workable interest-free banking structure in which case the model presented may perhaps serve as an initial working paper.

In the judgement of the present writer that eventuality has already come. History is inexorably moving to a direction in which even those who disagree will find themselves forced to concur. Whether that stage will occur before or after a devastating global Armageddon is not known. International conflicts and tensions are nothing more than external manifestations of internal tensions and conflicts generated by inequitable socio-economic arrangements, ultimately linked to the root-cause of it all, the institution of interest, and its diverse incurable consequences.

The main purpose of writing this book is to persuade men of goodwill around the globe to come forward and liberate reason from the chains of orthodoxy, and rationality from the shackles of sophistry, so that man is emancipated as much from the perpetual tyranny of exploitation as from the fear of his extinction. Let us turn to cold reasoning and unemotional analysis to enable ourselves to locate the cause of various cancerous growths in the economy and how these can be cured, which may make preparing for star war eventualities entirely unnecessary. Even capitalistic economics must concede, however concerned it may be with the perpetuation of exploitative purpose of capital, that even this has got to have a secondary place compared to the survival of mankind.

Can Growth Be Continuous?

A capitalistic economist, even when he may be willing

to outgrow the shibboleths that his discipline has coined for perpetuation of the institution of interest, may find some difficulty in accepting the view that continuous growth is possible after interest and statutory reserve have been thrown overboard. He may be willing to concede that after zero rate of interest is established, the rate of growth of the economy will reach a level of at least twice of what it was before the operation of shift-over started. But that this pace of growth can be kept up indefinitely will appear doubtful to him. Besides the inherent conflict between growth and stability which trade cycles have brought home to him, he can point out real constraints like labour shortage, or high wages or short supplies or even depletion of certain critically important raw materials or markets for finished goods.

Leaving aside the issue of real constraints for a moment, so far as perpetual recurrence of a downturn is concerned, it is a function of credit constraint. The model of interest-free banking that has been presented excludes precisely this very constraint.

Trade cycle is a very complex subject and cannot possibly be dealt with adequately as a subordinate side-issue in a small book. *Man and Money* devotes two chapters to this issue wherein it has been argued at length why trade cycles cannot survive the abolition of interest and bank reserves. Contracting the argument to a sentence, we may say that with the extinction of credit constraint, occasioned in the main by interest and bank reserve, the monetary compulsion of a down-turn ceases to exist. So far as non-monetary explanations of the trade cycle are concerned, so long as there is equilibrium between saving and investment at the *ex-ante level,* and the interest-free and reserve-free model by definition ensures it, there cannot be any disequilibrium between production and consumption, demand and supply, factor costs and prices. Once Say's Law gets resurrected the question of *general* shrinking of market for finished products ceases to exist. This does not amount to saying that changes in the pattern of demand will not occur. But if there is shortfall in demand of certain products, there will be pro-rata increase in demand for some other products, and consistent realignment of productive facilities, with the help of free credit, will always be able to attend to necessary correction. To sum up, neither from the monetary aspect nor from the real aspect, there is any occasion for an upper turning point to emerge and therefore for trade cycle to call a halt to consistent growth. The only conceivable possibility for a down-turn can emerge when human wants get satiated, not only in one country but all over the globe, of which for the present even a remote possibility is not discernible.

Let us examine this presentation in the context of specific real constraints pointed out by the critic. Let us assume that growth has reached a stage where either no more labour is available or is available at a cost which export industries cannot bear. Such a situation does not arise all at once. It casts its long shadow before it. There is no reason to believe that entrepreneurs will not strive to meet it by induction of suitable automotive processes. Stretching the argument to its ultimate possibilities, robots will increasingly take up much of the work now done by human labour. Increasing automation of productive processes will ensure that shortage of labour, or exceptional rise in wages will not call a halt to consistent growth. This however does not exclude the possibility that particular skills may on occasion be in short supply. Entrepreneurs will learn by experience which are the particular skills which they should impart under an in-service arrangement to ensure the unhindered growth of their enterprises. In the final analysis, it boils down to whether capital will be available to impart the principle of substitution in the labour market. The T.M.C.L. banking arrangement specifically ensures this availability.

If capital and technology can apply the principle of substitution in the labour market, these can be relied upon to do it with even greater success in the case of various commodity shortages which the critic visualizes.

It is unnecessary to repudiate the possibility of capital

being available and technology being unavailable. In the short term, as a general rule, technology is a purchasable item; in the long run, it is a product of research. If capital is available, both short term and long term possibilities of acquisition of technology co-exist. In exceptional cases, where technology is not purchasable, foreign equity participation will open the path to its availability.

The Problem of Flight of Capital

Yet another criticism can be levelled from the standpoint of capitalistic economics that if interest is reduced to zero, this will lead to flight of capital to countries which yield interest on deposits, counteracting the prosperity paradigm of the interest-free model. However deeply entrenched the view may be both in economic theory and public policy, it has seldom been able to win any support from objective reality and empirical evidence. When this non-conformity of objective reality and economic theory are subjected to analysis, we find that the theory is also devoid of any significant logic. It tends grossly to under-rate the real propellers of movement of capital which happen to be prospects of significantly gainful enterprise, stability of currency, and security of investment. As the interest-free banking with in-built fiscal balance, is calculated to quicken and strengthen these very propellers, the liklihood of movement of capital into the country would significantly outweigh the consideration of earning interest outside the country.

Tooke was perhaps the initiator of the theoretical argument in favour of interest elasticity of capital movement. At a later date, this reason was concisely stated by Bagehot in his verdict that "Loanable capital, like every other commodity, comes where there is most to be made of it."[158] Practical obstacle to actual working of the concept was pointed out by Goschen by saying that even a substantial difference of interest yielded only a small gain in comparison with the exchange risk.[159] The Bank of England had already reached that conclusion by 1857 when Weguelin, the Governor of the Bank, expressed his view that "raising of the rate of interest ... has not, in my view, any very material effect as regards the righting of the exchange."[160]

Hawtrey who has meticulously documented variations in bank rate in England and other countries over a period of an entire century, quite often finds the impact on the foreign exchange balances to be insignificant, and not any the less often even inverse of what it is regarded to be.[161] He, therefore, after evaluating various theoretical arguments in the light of the wealth of empirical evidence spread over a century reaches the conclusion: "There may be reasons for moving Bank rate either by big steps or by small .. the attraction of foreign funds ought not to be among them."[162]

When economics is confronted with objective repudiation of its theoretical posture, it prefers to give a new turn to its presentation without changing the substance of its stand. About 1920 the naivete of interest elasticity of gold and capital movement was replaced by deflationary effect produced by dear money through its dampening effect on investment which, by compressing consumers' income, tended to strengthen balance of payments position. In the 1920's this method of protecting foreign balances was so widely practiced that it landed the entire world by the end of the decade in the Great Depression. It was this experience which made Keynes exclaim: "Recently, practical bankers have learnt much, and one can almost hope that in Great Britain the technique of bank rate will never be used again to protect the foreign balances in conditions in which it is likely to cause unemployment at home."[163]

Apart from consistent failure to achieve its objective of winning support and strength for the foreign exchange position by adherence to the policy of raising the bank rate, there is a fundamental theoretical fault with the notion of producing deflationary effect with its help and thus strengthen balance of payments position. It is a surprise how capitalistic economics could slur over a yawning gap in the argument. A rise in rate of interest leads to deflationary consequence from the line of reasoning which begins from rise in interest, and proceeds successively to lower investment, therefore lower employment, therefore lower incomes, therefore lower pressure of demand for both consumptional and productive purposes, therefore lower pressure on imports, and therefore strengthening of balance of payments position. The line of argument completely overlooks the other side of the coin. Exactly in the measure in which investment will slacken, supplies will also dwindle. The faltering in demand will be accompanied definitionally, by a *pari passu* reduction in supplies. This means that not only demand for foreign goods will decrease, the capability of exporting goods to foreign markets will also decline in an identical measure, even if other countries did not resort to a similar deflationary policy.

Another argument advanced in the late 1920s to support the notion of a dear money policy was to discourage speculation. This is like justifying firing a Klashnikov to kill a fly. Credit control is entirely capable of denying loans for speculative purposes without raising the interest rate. Hawtrey refutes both these reasons for justifying raising the bank rate by saying whether it is speculation or improving the foreign exchange position, there is no escaping the consequence of "stopping prosperity".[164]

If economics were true to its purpose of human welfare, it would not so persistently stand by an institution which under all circumstances raises insuperable obstacles in the path of attainment of that goal. Every rise in interest tilts the scale in favour of possessive investments as against creative investments, every fall creates the opposite consequence of generating support for creative investments as against possessive investments. It is for the capitalistic economist to define the ultimate purpose of his discipline. Is it welfare of man or welfare of money he should strive for? In the former case, he should stand for enterprise and creative investment and in the latter for possessive savings. So far as Keynes is concerned, he took his decision a long time back. "If Enterprise is afoot" he wrote, "wealth accumulates whatever may be happening to Thrift; and if Enterprise is asleep, wealth decays whatever Thrift may be doing."[165]

To sum up, there is neither any logic nor any objective reality in the emphasis given by capitalistic economics to interest elasticity of international capital movement. Even in modern times, there is no semblance of empirical support for the notion that if interest is reduced to zero, capital will flow out of the country. It is true that the nature of evidence is indirect, as no country has hitherto practiced banking at zero rate of interest. Nevertheless, there are such wide variations in bank rate among various countries that if capital movement were as sensitive to interest as economic theory makes it out to be, capital would be depleted from low-interest contries and would overflow into high-interest countries. Looking up the bank rate in six of the more significant capitalistic countries during the decade of the 1970s *i.e.,* from 1971 to 1980, we find that average annual bank rate was 9.45 per cent in France, 4.8 per cent in West Germany, 6.12 per cent in Japan, 2.99 per cent in Switzerland, 11.45 per cent in U.K., and 9.45 per cent in U.S.A.[166] If capital really seeks higher interest rate, no capital should have been left in Switzerland and should have moved to U.K. where bank rate was almost four times higher, or at least moved to U.S.A. where it was more than three times higher. Identically, German capital should have moved out to France where it could earn almost twice as much interest, and Japanese capital should have moved to U.S.A. for 50 per cent higher return, or better still to U.K. for almost 100 per cent higher return. But no such movement of capital took place in any of these countries for this consideration which only establishes that zero rate of interest will remain an identically subsidiary consideration for exodus of capital compared with sound trade policies, suitable climate for enterprise and real investment, responsible budgetary policies, stable currency and security of investment. Since interest-free banking is potentially capable of providing all these things with far more assurance than any interest-oriented society, the question of exodus of capital can only be regarded in the words of Marx "a kindergarten story."

Answer to Socialist Critics

The socialist critic can raise two objections against this model of banking. Having been nurtured on the concept of regarding profit as the main instrument of exploitation, he cannot be persuaded to accept a model which relies on this very profit motive to generate productive expansionism to the limit of extinction of unemployment. What is worse from the socialist point of view is that the model leans on denationalization of most public sector ventures, and in particular the loss-generating ones, to induct efficiency into these under private enterprise, and thus provide, as the critic is likely to put it, further opportunity to the entrepreneurial class to amass additional profits.

The socialist critic may not be alone in making that observation. Much of liberal economic thought views with grave misgiving reliance on the entrepreneurial class to deliver productivity and efficient functioning at an acceptable cost. In fact, the tendency towards monopoly or at least oligopolic profits have led to evolution of concepts like Galbraithian wage and income policy, which would denude this class of many of its decision-making functions.

Even Islamic economics bears the stamp of this socialist and liberal point of view, and has hitherto abstained from underscoring the validity of profit motive, notwithstanding Quranic observation of *ahallallahul bai'a* (2:275) *i.e.*, Allah has permitted trade. This amounts to conceding that Islamic economists (including the present writer) have hitherto overlooked the priority that Islam confers on free enterprise.

Yet another objection can be raised from the socialist and liberal points of view that the proposed pattern of banking will only help the rich become richer and provide no relief to those who need it most. If a man has security worth Rs. 1.1 million and a counter-loan of Rs. 1,25,000, he can get a loan of a million rupees, and without interest to boot. But the one who has security worth Rs. 1,000 and only Rs. 50 in his pocket cannot get even a loan of Rs. 10,000.

We shall now attempt to answer these objections in the order in which these have been raised.

Exogenous Nature of Exploitation at Profit Level

In the classical model profits could not be exploitative. Competition was the theoretical lever which ensured equilibrium in factor costs in the system of free enterprise. The model is faultless except when applied to interest, which was assumed to be an equilibrating mechanism between saving and investment. As this part of the argument runs exactly parallel to the interaction of demand and supply in the determination of prices in the commodity market, few noticed the inelastic nature of the supply of savings, nor the alternative to investment in the purchase of debts, provided by interest, ensuring perpetual disequilibrium between saving and investment. In the confused projection of the theoretical argument even fewer noticed the role of reserve of banks as monetary scarcity instrument, which must result in outflow of advances suffering deduction compared with the inflow of deposits. This contrived disequilibrium between saving and investment jointly bolstered by interest and statutory reserve, has virtually paralysed the classical model, as it overlooked the neutralizing impact of these institutional arrangements on the equilibrating propensity of the market forces, the hidden hand as it was called.

If we could devise a credit structure which declines to lean on either interest or statutory reserve, a "sea-change" occurs at the level of re-activating of market forces which are completely capable of equilibrating demand and supply both in the product and factor markets, restoring potency to Say's Law, and ensuring full employment at stable prices.

It is the failure to understand this reality, which led Marx to misconstruction of his surplus value concept. He did not realize that while exploitative role played by interest was endemic and co-extensive with its own being and therefore completely in accord with his surplus value concept, the exploitation exhibited by profit and rent was exogenous, transmitted to these by the exploitative and constrictive role played by interest, and therefore exhibiting only partial eligibility for inclusion in surplus value.

Confining ourselves to profit which is the point under attack, we have to look at it not with the eyes of Marx or Mao Tse Tung but those of Gorbachev and Deng Xiaoping. The socialist experiment in Russia and China has proved without a shadow of doubt that without activating profit motive efficient functioning of economic arrangements cannot be ensured. Perhaps the most telling proof of the creativity of the profit motive is the difference in productivity between private plots and socialized agriculture in Russia. On the basis of authentic Soviet publications, Hedrick Smith has computed that out of private plots, which form one per cent of total agricultural land in Russia, come $32.5 billion worth of products, which form 27 per cent of the total agricultural output of Russia.[167] So, that is the measure of productivity of the profit motive: It can multiply production 27 times.

Another equally compelling evidence of the productivity of profit motive and the snail-paced growth of public owned and centrally planned productive organization is provided by comparison between economies of Russia and Japan. While Russia spans across two continents, Japan is a small group of islands, the difference in area being more than 56 to 1. Russia is inordinately endowed with all varieties of mineral wealth; Japan is exceptionally devoid of it. Japan has a population almost one third that of Russia, and both countries started their development more or less about the same time. Yet Japan's G.N.P. has already crossed over that of Soviet Russia.[168] Sometimes facts speak louder than any logic.

Besides the practical necessity of recognizing profit as a necessary reward for imparting efficiency into the productive process Marx was, even on theoretical ground, in error, in excluding labour of organization and supervision as falling outside the scope of labour theory of value. If it is socially necessary labour, it has to be recognized as productive labour. The correct posture in the matter of this pre-classical doctrine is the one subscribed to by Keynes. He writes: "It is preferable to regard labour, including of course, the personal services of the entrepreneur and his assistants, as the sole factor of production, operating in a given environment of technique, natural resources, capital equipment and effective demand."[169] To exclude the labour of enterprise from its original habitat of labour theory of value, and to push it into a substantially alien category of surplus value, is to put the cart before the horse and thus virtually depriving both of their innate mobility.

This is not to say that profits do not upraise their level well beyond the appropriate reward of the labour of enterprise. Far from it. It is not only a matter of everyday experience but many detailed studies of what Galbraith calls the planning sector persuade us to acknowledge that profits include a component of exploitation and of surplus value. It is the business of the theoretical economist to separate the chaff from the grain and spell out why inordinate quantity of chaff gets mixed up with grain. The classicists did not visualize the emergence of this exploitative component in profits on account of their assumption of a competitive market, and allowed for its emergence only under monopolistic conditions. In 1932-33, E.H. Chamberlain and Joan Robinson repudiated the notions of both competition and monopoly, leading to a widespread recognition that the markets were neither purely competitive nor fully monopolized, but bore the characteristics of both competition and monopoly. These were imperfectly competitive.

It is this imperfection in the competitive competence of the market which is responsible for the exploitative component of profit. We need to go behind the existence of this imperfection to find out the reason for its emergence and whether or not we have any remedy which can cure it, before we can decide on unexceptionable eligibility of profit for inclusion in the labour theory of value.

In conformity with the general slant of economics to

overlook the depredatory impact and consequences of the institution of interest, all kinds of secondary explanations for market distortions are available. The growth of oligopoly, the trend of profit concentration, along with a significant hardening of the labour market are cases in which, except for ever-widening range of controls euphemistically called income policy, no remedy suggests itself to current progressive thinking in economics.

Few have thought fit to go into the trend towards quasi-monopolistic reaction at the level of enterprise and labour as a necessary consequence of the monopoly price charged by capital, although the dominant role played by this factor could not possibly fail to kindle what Galbraith has called in a different context, countervailing power in enterprise and labour. If capital enables itself to charge a monopoly price by generating artificial scarcity through bank reserve, other factors have to strive hard to ensure their adequate share of the national income. It is this effort that has forced enterprise to achieve comparable strength through attaining, to the limit of possibility, the oligopolic status, just as the inherent exploitation of capital, and the acquired oligopolic exploitation of enterprise force labour to attain comparable strength through intensification of trade union organization, in its struggle for its share of the sun-shine.

What is fair profit, and which is the level after which exploitative profits begin are questions to which answers can only be given by a free and competitive market. Since such a market can exist only in an environment in which competition is liberated from the constrictive consequence of statutory reserve and emancipated from the exploitative impact of interest and since both these conditions are non-existent, an empirically supported answer cannot possibly be given.

At the deductive level, it has never been questioned that interest has a hardening impact on the profit level. Every loan on interest increases hazards of enterprise. If we were to expect enterprise to upraise its profit, besides recovery of interest, by only one half of the cost of capital, it will involve excess in profits of 1-1/2 times the level of interest rate. If profit confines itself to the recovery of interest only, it means it is charging nothing for the increase in hazards which interest on loan capital has imposed on it. This would be as unrealistic as it would be unlikely to happen, except when slump forces down the reward of enterprise itself.

The lowest estimate of relationship between interest and profit and of a fair rate of profit was given by Adam Smith. Cassel tells that according to Adam Smith, in his time, double interest was considered a fair rate of profit.[170] The usury limit being 5 per cent for the greater part of the eighteenth century[171] during which Adam Smith lived, fair profit according to the estimation of his time comes to 10%. With deepening depredation of loan capital, horizontally as well as vertically, both the rate of interest and the level of multiples of interest as essential anticipatory profit has been rising. Lorie Tarshis does not give the exact measure of these multiples, but states that in every industrial venture "the allowance for risk is frequently very high—perhaps a multiple of the interest rate."[172] According to Hawtrey, an industrialist, keeping in view maintenance and depreciation will seek a probable yield likely to vary between 2-1/2 and 5 multiples of interest.[173] According to Bronfenbrenner, necessary anticipatory profit fluctuates around three multiples of the going rate of interest.[174] The present author undertook an exercise to determine the exact level of profit as multiple of interest in U.S.A. from 1945 to 1979 from national income accounts of the country. Though the tabulation has been made at five year intervals, the result is unlikely to vary significantly if every year had been taken into account. According to this calculation, despite wide variations from year to year, weighted average of profits in relation to interest during this 35 years period comes to 3.68 multiples of net interest,[175] lending some empirical support to the theoretical enunciation of above economists.

This looks like almost twice of what would have been regarded fair profit in Adam Smith's time. As a very rough approximation we can say that one-half of the going level of profits is the wages of enterprise, which on account of its social necessity eminently deserves to fall in the category of labour theory of value. The other half is partly dictated by the institution of interest and the magnification of risk which is its necessary consequence, and partly occasioned by imperfection of competition. This second half obviously falls in the category of surplus value. So, we can neither denounce profit as entirely exploitative, nor can we justify it in its entirety as wages of enterprise. In spite of this reality the grain and the chaff are separable. Whatever measure of exploitation we witness in profit does not inhere in it. It is transmitted to it, in fact imposed on it, partly by interest and partly by imperfect competition both of which are sustained by artificially manipulated scarcity of capital, through the device of bank reserve.

It is in this context that we have to examine the validity or otherwise of the interest-free banking model that is under examination. Can it cleanse profit of its exploitative content? It is on the answer to this question that the final decision, in the context of the objection under reply, should be reached.

One-half of the exploitative content of profit is eliminated, by definition, by the mere extinction of interest. There is neither any interest nor any magnification of risk on this account for which enterprise regards itself justified to upraise the level of profit. So, the transmission of exploitation from interest to profit ceases with the elimination of the former. This is a point already made both by Keynes and some of the Keynesians, though perhaps not with as much clarity as it deserves to be made. Keynes wrote: "If I am right in supposing it to be comparatively easy to make capital goods so abundant that the marginal efficiency of capital is zero, this may be the most sensible way of getting rid of the many objectionable features of capitalism."[176] Kurihara elaborates: "For if the rate of interest is zero, the volume of investment will be pushed to the point where the marginal efficiency of capital becomes zero, with the result that the owner of capital can no longer earn pure interest any more than a competitive firm can earn 'pure profit' in the long run."[177]

It is true that a 'competitive firm' cannot earn 'pure profit' or profit beyond the legitimate reward of enterprise. But how can the emergence of competitive firm be ensured? Zero rate of interest in this context assumes a secondary position compared to extinction of bank reserve. It is only in the context of elimination of bank reserve that artificial scarcity of capital can be extinguished. Imperfection of competition cannot end unless supply of capital is made to assume equilibrium with the demand of capital at zero rate of interest. Actually, it is this bank reserve which is responsible for disparity between saving and investment in this interest-ridden economy. If we reduce interest to zero, and take no step to demolish artificial curtailment of the supply of saving, this disparity will only be accentuated.

But once we do away with bank reserve, we open the door to equilibrium between saving and investment and between demand and supply of capital at zero rate of interest. This is the necessary pre-condition to the emergence of the "competitive firm", enabling extinction of that portion of exploitative profit which is provided by imperfect competition.

To sum up, in an interest-free and bank-reserve-free banking arrangement, both the constituents of exploitative component of profit cease to exist. Neither interest nor its risk magnifying impact which forces profit to upraise its level will survive, eliminating one half of its exploitative component, and the other half is taken care of by extinction of statutory reserve, activating productive competition to a level in which oligopolic profit cannot survive.

Once this pincer movement cleanses profit of its entire exploitative component, it becomes completely eligible for inclusion in the labour theory of value. It is to this profit oriented enterprise that the interest-free model under discussion entrusts the task of productive expansionism and efficient utilization of resources available in a given context. It does not lead to widening of the area of exploitation as the critic from his pre-conceived doctrinaire point of view is forced to visualize, but to complete elimination of even the measure of exploitation which exists in profit at the time. It simultaneously excludes the necessity of resorting to diverse controls which have an inherent tendency to expand their area of operation, till we land ourselves in a network of bureaucratic management of the economy characterized by sloth, indifference and inefficiency.

Contribution of Interest-Free Model in Elimination of Poverty

The second adverse observation likely to be made by a socialist critic is that the model, far from ameliorating the lot of the masses, provides capital resources to those who already have them in the shape of collateral and counter-loan, and denies them to those who do not possess them. This will make the rich, richer and the poor, poorer.

While the premise is correct the conclusion is entirely incorrect. It is true that loans cannot be advanced to people who possess neither the requisite collateral nor the requisite counter-loan, though some manipulation in the latter condition is possible, subject to monetary policy of the country, by deducting counter-loan from the loan advanced, no such relief is possible in the matter of collateral. It is necessary to remind the critic that this is a model for a viable and profitable interest-free banking system and lays no claim to be regarded as a susbtitute for charity houses.

But it does something far more revolutionary for the have-nots than any collection of charity houses can do. By eliminating unemployment, it creates conditions in which charity houses should become redundant. The most pervasive cause for poverty and privation is that a significant percentage of people, in particular those who belong to the lower rungs of the social structure, can either find no employment, or can only engage themselves in some vocation on a part-time basis. This is the fundamental cause of widespread poverty. Social security apparatus of developed countries, howsoever laudable it may be from a charitable point of view, is no substitute for employment. Men seek work not only because it gives them a living, but also because it is a physical and emotional need of all healthy men. Social security may act as hush-money for the survival of the capitalistic system, but is no substitute for giving gainful employment to all.

Productive expansionism built into the interest-free banking model ensures extinction of unemployment, and provides gainful employment for every one who can do some kind of useful work. Having made this revolutionary contribution to elimination of poverty, it does not regard itself called upon to give loans to even those who do not possess any collateral. It is not necessary that every one may come forward to self-employ himself. If some one has the necessary collateral and counter-loan, let him do that as well. If not, let him seek a job, work hard at it, save necessary means of securing a loan, and then let him have the satisfaction of becoming his own boss. Till that happens, he has to content himself with a job which the market is prepared to offer to him.

The basic contribution that interest-free banking makes in the direction of elimination of poverty is that it enables economy to provide gainful employment to all, and the magnitude of this contribution cannot be clouded by its inability to give loans to all.

So far as the specific example given by the critic is concerned even in this area there is a significant improvement in the availability of credit. A person with collateral worth Rs. 1000 and only Rs. 50 as cash in his pocket of course cannot get a loan of Rs. 10,000. Under the present banking arrangements in Pakistan, he can get a loan of Rs. 600 or thereabout at 17 or 18 per cent interest. Under TMCL arrangement, he could get Rs. 910 as loan if he had Rs. 113 to give as counter-loan. Since he has only Rs. 50 for this purpose, Rs. 63 will have to be deducted from his loan for adjustment towards his counter-loan. This means, he can get a loan of Rs. 857 without interest, as against Rs. 600 at 17% interest. The difference between the two positions is not as insignificant as the critic appears to regard it.

Objection of the Panel of Experts

The most interesting part of the story is that religious orthodoxy which pays consistent lip sympathy to Islam's prohibition of interest, while according acceptance to every subterfuge that perpetuates it, does not appear to be in any hurry to accept a genuine interest-free structure envisaged by this model. The Council of Islamic Ideology in Pakistan appointed a Panel of Economists and Bankers in November 1977 to advise it on the methodology of eliminating interest. The TMCL concept was then in a rudimentary form in which it assumed responsibility of answering only the first of the ten problems spelled out in Chapter II which any interest-free banking structure has got to resolve before it can establish its workability. It would have been understandable if the Panel hesitated in according acceptance to it on account of the various issues which emerge on account of adoption of the model, and were unanswerd at that time. The Panel, however, never went that far in evaluating the model and confined itself to admitting its "potential usefulness" though expressing uncertainty regarding "whether this method would be in conformity with the *shari'ah.*"[178]

Now this was an aspect of evaluation which did not fall within the purview of the Panel of Economists and Bankers as the very name of the Panel indicates. The real obstacle was that by the nature of their training and predilection the members were only concerned with retaining the substance of interest under some garb which may appear plausible to *shari'ah* rather than eliminating it. Their Report entitled *The Elimination of Interest from the Economy*[179] is really an exercise in substitution rather than elimination.

A single sentence is enough to reflect the general approach of the Panel in the matter of interest. Enumerating its shortcomings, it observes, "a fixed interest rate can also be unjust to the lender of money in case the entrepreneur using this money earns a profit quite out of proportion to what he pays by way of interest."[180]

Their general approach in recommending various substitutes was to raise the reward of capital at the cost of enterprise. The one which won eventual acceptance at the policy-making level is reproduced below:

"A business firm needs finance from a bank ... Instead of ... making an advance, the bank under an arrangement with the firm concerned may purchase/import the commodity on its own account and sell it to the firm at a price, to be settled in advance, which includes a mark-up over the cost price for a reasonable profit margin for the bank. Payment from the firm would be receivable by the bank after the agreed period."[181]

Under the thin garb of a business transaction, a loan of money earns a mark-up of "a reasonable profit margin" which is "settled in advance" and which is payable "after the agreed period". So, an agreed amount is advanced by a bank to a borrower, even though in the shape of goods that he needs, for an agreed period, on a pre-determined level of mark-up, and that precisely boils down to what interest constitutes.

In actual functioning, even the theoretical veneer of a business transaction is laid aside. The borrower receives the amount, as heretofore, agrees to pay a "mark-up" at a specified level, "after the agreed period". The only difference is elimination of the word "interest", though its level has been raised from 14% to 17% or above. We now claim that we have abolished interest. Indeed, we have, so far as the word "interest" is concerned; otherwise, we have only raised its level by three percentage points.

It was in the context of this conviction that the substance of interest should not be eliminated and only its form should be changed in a manner that it should appear to be a business transaction rather than a loan, that the Panel gave consideration to TMCL concept. Though even in its preliminary form in which it was available to the Panel, it was capable of promising elimination of interest, that prescisely became the reason why it could not be accepted. But this real reason could not be given. Therefore, after explaining the TMCL concept the Report made the following observation:

"It may be pointed out that the Panel is not certain whether this method would be in conformity with *shari'ah.* It has been suggested here in view of its potential usefulness for consideration of the Council subject to its permissibility under the *shari'ah.*"[182]

Posture of The Council of Islamic Ideology

The present author wrote his note of dissent to the Report of the Panel, which has since been published,[183] in which he showed how various proposals made by the Panel amounted to an effort to retain interest under some guise, and answered the various objections that could be raised to the TMCL concept from the point of view of the *shari'ah* to which we shall revert in a while.

This latter portion of the Note of Dissent won qualified acceptance from the Council of Islamic Ideology which observed after explaining the TMCL concept, that "if it is desired that provision may be made for providing personal loans to people of small means, then instead of the above stipulations the banks may adopt it as a principle that they would provide loans for personal and non-productive purposes only to those persons who already hold accounts with them..." The Council also expressed "the view that it would not be correct to use this method by way of a permanent alternative system to the interest-based system."[184]

There are two interesting facets of these observations of the Council of Islamic Ideology. One is that counter-loan is not to be advanced at the time of securing a loan, but the borrower should already hold a suitable account with the bank, presumably commensurate with the dimension and period of the loan that is demanded. If it is to avoid conditional lending, a point we shall look into after a moment, then the condition of counter-loan is no worse than the condition of giving loans "only to those persons who already hold accounts." The sophistication introduced only serves to hide the reality of a counter-loan, and virtually amounts to advising pretension of its non-existence.

The second equally interesting observation is that while the system is good enough for personal loans, it is not good enough for other varieties of loans. We already know why the exact opposite of it corresponds to the correct position. But the point here is that the Council does not explain why what is good for the goose becomes unacceptable for the gander. It has not been deemed necessary to divulge either any techincal or any moral grounds for making this differentiation.

The result is that the Council, by and large, supports adoption of various subterfuges for retention of interest, but cannot give unqualified support to the only way in which it can be eliminated.

Answers to Fundamentalists' Objections to TMCL Concept

The fundamentalists, it must be conceded, labour under certain difficulties, in the matter of acceptance of the TMCL concept. It is therefore necessary to examine these difficulties and evaluate whether any of these really bars the acceptance of the only concept available so far with whose help it is possible to introduce interest-free banking.

The first difficulty is the one mentioned earlier regarding prohibition of conditional loans. For instance, there is a *hadith* narrated by Abdullah Bin Umar saying "whoever advances a loan should not make it conditional with the exception of return of the loan."[185] Allama Wahid-uz-Zaman explaining the meaning of this *hadith* says that a lender should not impose any condition which confers any advantage on the lender."[186] Under TMCL concept exactly identical loan values are exchanged and no advantage exceeding the loan value received is conferred by the borrower upon the lender. Actually, both the parties are simultaneously lenders as well as borrowers, and there is nothing that one lends to the other which is any the less or more than either of them borrows from the other. Unless the borrower is forced to give some variety of advantage to the lender in addition to the loan value he receives, the arrangement cannot be called conditional loan of a variety which is not permissible.

Even this interpretation has to be further diluted keeping in view the fact of undisputed legitimacy available in the case of *mudarabah* wherein the condition of a share in the profits is imposed on the *mudarib* by *rabbal-mal*. Profits being indeterminate and therefore uncertain, imposition of the condition of sharing the profit, in addition to return of the loan, is considered thoroughly legitimate. Keeping this permissibility in view, only such a conditional loan is prohibited wherein a condition of specific and determinate advantage is imposed by the lender in his favour. No such advantage forms a part of the counter-loan concept. Both the lender and the borrower exchange exactly equal loan values, and profit made or loss incurred by either party cannot be passed on to the other. As no advantage of a *specific and determinate* variety accrues to the lender, the concept falls outside the range of conditional loan of a variety which is prohibited.

Another point of attack from the fundamentalist point of view is the *hadith* which prohibits "sale of a debt in exchange for another debt."[187] Imam Malik after narrating the *hadith* explains its meaning by saying: "A person sells cloth or some other goods on the promise of payment by the purchaser after a month. A month passes and the buyer, being unable to make the payment, asks the seller of goods to sell his debt of one month for a debt of two months, and *raise the quantum of debt.* This is the sale of debt in exchange for another debt."[188](italics added)

Tabari in his *Tafseer* regards it as the general pattern of credit that was prevalent during *Jahilyya.* He explains the meaning of prohibition of *riba* in the *Quran* by saying "*La ta'kulu alriba fi Islamikum ba'da iz hadakum lahu kama kuntum ta'klunahu fi jahilyyatikum wa kana akluhum zalika fi jahilyyatihim anna alrajulu minhum kana yakunu lahu ala alrajuli malun ila ajalin fa iza hallal ajalu talabahu min saha bahi fa yaqulu lahu allazi alaihil malu akhkhir anni dainaka wa azeeduka ala malika.* "[189] Rendered into English it means, "Do not claim interest after acceptance of Islam as you used to do during *Jahilyya.* The method was that a person had a claim of an amount of money after a particular date against another person. When the time for payment came, the creditor would claim the payment from the debtor, on which the latter would request for extension in the period for payment against *increase in the amount of debt.*" (italics added)

This in effect was the exchange of an unpaid debt for a higher debt payable after a stipulated period of time. Sayyed Qutab quotes Qatada to explain how it emerged and what shape it took. "*Inna riba ahlal jahilyyati yabi'ul rajulu ila ajalin musamma fa iza hallal 'ajulu wa lam yakun 'inda sahibihi qadaun zadahu wa akhara 'anhu*".[189-A] Translated into English it means, "Interest during *Jahilyya* emerged when a person sold something to another person on credit for a defined time. When the time for payment came and the debtor did not settle the claim, *the amount of debt was increased* against extension in the time for repayment." (italics added) This was the exchange of one debt for another which the Holy Prophet prohibited, as it was only a method of extracting interest from the debtor.

E.W. Lane's *An Arabic English Lexicon,* gives the following meaning of *bai'al-kali bil kali i.e.,* sale of debt for a debt:

"A type of credit sales in which on the date of the discharge of the debt the debtor seeks extension with the promise to pay something in addition. In fact the amount of debt is sold to the debtor for some profit. What is meant by this is, a man's buying a thing on credit for certain period and when the period of payment comes and he does not find anything to pay, he says to the creditor: sell it to me on credit for a further period *for something additional...*".[190] (italics added)

It is obvious that this prohibition does not apply to the

counter-loan concept as no rise in the quantum of counter-loan compared with the loan advanced is stipulated. Actually, in such cases, the fundamentalists a little too often confuse the form with the substance, somehow giving greater value to the shell than the kernel. It could be a good guidance for us if we could, following the bidding of the Holy Prophet to seek knowledge even though it may be in China, give some thought to a profound Biblical observation to the effect that "it is the word that killeth and the spirit that kindleth life."[191] The spirit behind both these prohibitions is to exclude the possibility of certain varieties of subterfuges for interest. Counter-loan concept, far from providing yet another subterfuge for interest, is the only one capable of exterminating interest, and the only one capable of avoiding the necessity of resorting to subterfuges of this or any other variety. While "the word" does not prohibit the concept, "the spirit" compells its acceptance.

Yet another objection has been raised with reference to *al-Mughni,* wherein it is stated that if a lender gets advantage in extending a loan, it becomes usury.[192] As we have already discussed, advantage in this context always means specific and determinate advantage. If we do not dilute the meaning by this qualifying phrase, then even *mudarabah* will fall in the prohibited category. If sharing of profit by the lender besides recovery of capital from the borrower is accepted as legitimate in a *mudarabah* arrangement, and this advantage has never been regarded usurious, because the advantage is indeterminate depending on the measure of success that attends a particular enterprise, then counter-loan concept is even more worthy of acceptance. Under this arrangement neither the borrower nor the lender gets any determinate advantage from each other; they only exchange equivalent possibility of earning a profit, whether they will actually do so depends on the quality of their respective productive effort.

Identical is the reply to an objection based on yet another *hadith* to the effect that every debt which is advantageous (for the lender) is usurious.[193] The only difference is that

Swad bin Mus'ab, the narrator of this *hadith* is not regarded reliable.[194] Maulana Maudoodi concurs in that evaluation.[195]

This is all that can be said against the concept from the orthodox point of view. None of the prohibitive *ahadith* hits the concept. Actually, the concept never existed at the time of the Holy Prophet. As a matter of fact, it did not exist before 1960.[196] He could not therefore express any opinion on a non-existing concept. He was prohibiting various varieties of subterfuges for interest and counter-loan concept is no subterfuge at all. It declines to touch interest even with a pair of tongs.

TMCL Concept Is Institutionalization of Qard Hasan

If we search the vocabulary of the religion of Islam for a term to which the concept approximates, it is, to all intents and purposes, *qard hasan*. The definition given of *qard hasan* is "A loan with the stipulation to return the principal sum in the future without any increase."[197] That precisely is what banks will do under TMCL arrangement: they will advance loans "with the stipulation to return the principal sum in the future without any increase." True, this loan will be matched by a counter-loan which also falls within the strict boundary of *qard hasan*. The only question left to be answered is whether one can advance *qard hasan* and recieve *qard hasan* from the same person simultaneously. It would be unrealistic to expect *ahadith* to give any direct guidance in the matter. But surprizingly the Quran gives the reply by posing an identical question "*Hal jazaul ihsan illal ihsan.*"[198] "Is there any reward for Good other than Good?" As every one familiar with Arabic knows the word *Ihsan*, translated here as good, comes from the same root from which word *hasan* in *qard hasan* comes. Limiting the wide meaning of the verse to the issue in hand, the Quran appears to accord complete approval to give *qard hasan* and receive *qard hasan* as its reward. Allah in giving this permission regards it as His bounty, because this verse is immediately followed by the verse, "*Fabi ayyi ala'i rabbikuma tokazziban.*"[199] "Then which of the favours of your Lord will ye deny?"

Let us not deny this special favour of the Lord in giving us this go-ahead singal. In the language of the Quran, all the 45 Muslim countries are in a state of "war with Allah and His Apostle." All the various facets of our degredation emanate from our collective unconcern with the magnitude of meaning contained in this verse reflected in our half-hearted intellectual efforts to cope with the issue of devising an interest-free banking structure, to enable ourselves to have a cease-fire with both. If after fourteen centuries, a genuine all-embracing interest-free alternative basis of banking has emerged, it appears necessary to receive it with both our hands and hearts so that we can arrange a cease-fire with Allah and His Prophet.

Let us suppose that the verse of the Quran according approval to the counter-loan basis of banking did not exist, and the *ahadith* that have been quoted to raise doubts about its permissibility, were genuinely prohibitive, even then, our response should be positive. After all arranging a ceasefire with Allah and His Prophet has got to have precedence over every other consideration. On this issue, the guidance of Islamic *fiqh* is unequivocal. One of its principles is to the effect that "when the removal of a great damage is not possible without accepting a smaller damage, recourse can be made to that line of action."[200] Similarly, Imam Ibn Taymiyyah points out, "If an evil cannot be rooted out completely, it should be removed to the limit of possibility."[201]

If the objections have any validity, let the objectors evolve a substitute for interest which is shorn of the shortcomings that are being pointed out. Counter-loan concept does not stop any one from either improving upon this concept or devising a better alternative. It only pleads that till such an alternative emerges, we should shift over to this concept so that we can arrange a cease-fire with Allah and His Prophet.

What is the option if we do not accept the TMCL concept? We continue with our game of subterfuge under the pseudonyms of mark-up, leasing, etc., which means we continue practicing interest, and continue pretending that we have abolished it. Perhaps, we may like to heed what Prophet Eisa (Jesus Christ) has said on the subject of preferring pretension to the abolition of evil on flimsy excuses. Addressing the Pharisees who were doing it he said, "Ye blind guides, which strain at a gnat, and swallow a camel."[202]

Fortunately, there is no doubt about the permissibility of the concept from the Islamic point of view, and therefore, we neither need to swallow a camel nor strain at a gnat. None of the *ahadith* relates to this concept, much less express disapproval for it. The Quran gives such unbounded, and in its own inimitable language "bountiful", approval to it, that except for various varieties of bias, discussed in the first chapter, nothing stands in the way. So far as bias is concerned the injunction of the Holy Quran is "Confound not truth with falsehood..."[203]

REFERENCES AND NOTES

1. Homer, Sidney, *A History of Interest Rates,* Rutgers University Press, 1977, p. 17
2. *The Jewish Encyclopaedia,* New York, 1905, Vol. 12, p. 389.
3. *Encyclopaedia of Religion and Ethics,* Edinburgh, 1921, Vol. 12, pp. 549-50.
4. Keynes, *General Theory of employment Interest and Inoney* p. 351.
5. *Ibid,* pp. 374-6.
6. *Ibid.,* pp. 308-9.
7. Baron, *A Social and Religious History of the Jews,* New York, 1958, Vol. I, p. 105.
8. *The Jewish Encyclopaedia,* cit. op., Vol. XII p. 390.
9. Homer, Sidney, *A History of Interest Rates,* cit. op. p. 88.
10. al-Shaukani, *Nail al-Autar,* Vol. 5, p. 301.
11. For a detailed evaluation of various devices suggested by the Panel of Experts in Pakistan, see the present writer's Urdu work *Sood Ki Mutabadil Asas.* Institute of Islamic Culture. Lahore, 1986,
12. *The Economist,* London, Oct. 26, 1985, p. 77.
13. Gide and Rist, *A History of Economic Doctrines,* (Harrop) London, 1953, p. 322.
14. *Ibid.,* pp. 314-26.
15. *International Financial Statistics Yearbook* 1979 by I.M.F. p. 392, read with identical publication for 1984, p. 555.
16. *World Development Report,* 1985, by World Bank, p. 175.
17. *Yearbook of Labour Statistics,* 1981, by I.L.O., p. 325
18. *World Development Report,* 1985 by World Bank, p. 175
19. Robinson, Joan, *Economic Heresies,* New York, 1971, p. 90
20. Harrod, R.F., *Towards A Dynamic Economics,* Macmillan, London, 1956, pp. 136-9.
21. Meade, J.E., *Economic Analysis and Policy,* O.U.P. 1950, p. 52.
22. Wernette, John Philip, *Financing Full Employment,* Harvard University Press, Cambridge, Massachusettes, 1945, p. 33.
23. Lerner, Abba, P., *Economics of Unemployment,* Kogakusha, Tokyo, 1951, p. 8.
24. Kurihara, K.K., *Monetary Theory and Public Policy,* Allen and Unwin, London, 1951, p. 36.
25. Wernette, John Philip, *Financing Full Employment,* cit. op. p. 31.
26. Vickrey, William S., "Stability Through Inflation" in Kurihara's *Post Keynesian Economics,* Allen and Unwin, London, 1955, p. 119.
27. *The Elimination of Interest from the Economy,*1980, State Bank of Pakistan Press.
28. Myrdal, Gunnar, *Against The Stream,* Pantheon, New York, 1973, p. 315.
29. *Ibid.,* p. 55.
30. Haberler, Gottfried von, *Prosperity and Depression,* Geneva, 1939, p. 195.
31. Lutz, Vera and Friedrich, *The Theory of Investment of the Firm, Princeton, 1951, p. 237.*
32. Samuelson, Paul A., *Economics,* 10th Edition, Mcgraw Hill Kogakusha, Tokyo, 1976, p. 817.
33. *Ibid.,* p. 822.
34. *Ibid.,* p. 614.
35. Myrdal, Gunnar, *Against the Stream,* cit. op. p. 54.
36. *Ibid.,* p. 58.
37. *Ibid.,* p. 2.

38. *Ibid.*, pp. 60-61.
39. Shah, Sayed Yaqub, *Chand Ma'ashi Masail aur Islam,* Institute of Islamic Culture, Lahore, 1967.
40. Myrdal, Gunnar, *Against the Stream,* cit. op. p. 61.
41. *General Theory,* cit. op. p. 298.
42. Bohm Bawerk, *Positive Theory of Capital,* London, 1891, p. 237.
43. *Ibid.*, p. 238.
44. *Ibid.*, p. 250.
45. *Ibid.*, p. 250.
46. *The Quran,* 2:275.
47. For details, see *Man and Money,* Chapter IX, Section 4.
48. Keynes, *General Theory.* cit. op. p. 375.
49. *Ibid.*, pp. 322-23, and 326-28.
50. *Ibid.*, It is 1-1/2 to 2 per cent on p. 208 and 2 to 2-1/2 per cent on p. 219.
51. *Ibid.*, p. 242.
52. *Ibid.*, p. 202.
53. *Ibid.*, p. 167.
54. *Ibid.*, p. 207.
55. *Ibid.*, Footnote No. 1 on p. 167.
56. *Ibid.*, p. 207.
57. *The Quran,* 2:275.
58. For a detailed repudiation of the theory see *Man and Money,* Chapter VIII, Section 7.
59. For exact figures and detailed analysis, *Man and Money,* Chap. III, Sec. 13.
60. Keynes, *General Theory,* cit. op. p. 376.
61. Percentages in the case of both countries worked out from figures given in *International Financial Statistics Year-book* for 1984 by I.M.F.
62. Wicksell, Knut, *Interest and Prices,* Macmillan, London, 1936, p. 120.
63. *Ibid.*, p XXVIII
64. Wicksell, *Selected Papers on Economic Theory,* George Allen & Unwin, London, 1958 p. 78.
65. *Ibid.*, p. 78.
66. Constraint of space does not permit going further into the issue. Those interested in detailed evaluation may look up Chapter VI of *Man and Money.*
67. The Quran, 2:275.
68. Keynes, *Treatise on Money,* Vol. II, London, 1934, p. 201.
69. *Ibid.*, p. 198.
70. Keynes, *General Theory,* cit. op., p. 322.
71. For elaboration, see Chapter I of *Man and Money,* entirely devoted to the issue.
72. Samuelson, *Economics, cit.op., p. 618.*
73. *Ibid.*, p. 606, f.n. 8.
74. Bohm-Bawerk, *Capital and Interest,* trans, Smart, london, 1890, p. 143.
75. *Ibid.*, p. 146.
76. Cassel, *Nature and Necesity of Interest,* Macmillan, London, 1903, p. 183-4.
77. *Ibid.*, p. 181.
78. Conard, Joseph W., *An Introduction to the Theory of Interest,* Berkeley, 1959, p. 12.
79. Schumpeter, Joseph A., *Ten Great Economists,* Allen & Unwin, London, 1951, pp. 179-80.
80. *e.g.*, Keynes and Harrod and many more. This may have been a contributory reason why Keynes and Harrod could write the exceptionally illuminating concluding chapters of their more distinghished books, *viz.*, *General Theory* and *Dynamic Economics* respectively.
81. Marx, *Capital,* Progress Publishers, Moscow, 1965, Vol.I p. 164.
82. *Ibid.*, Vol. I, p. 192, f.n.1.
83. *Ibid.*, Vol.I, p. 184.
84. *Ibid.*, Vol. I, p. 185.

85. Tariq, *Speeches and Statements of Iqbal,* p. 4.
86. *Ibid.,* p. 8.
87. *Iqbal's Letters to Jinnah, p. 17.*
88. *Ibid.,* p. 18.
89. *Ibid.,* p. 19.
90. *Ibid.,* p. 6.
91. From English translation of *Javid Nama* by the present writer, entitled *Pilgrimage of Enternity.* All subsequent translations from *Javid Nama* are also from the same book.
92. First published in 1946.
93. *Annual Report State Bank of Paksitan,* 1986-7, p. 154.
94. *Ibid.,* Statistical Annexure, p. 31.
95. *Ibid.,* Statistical Annexure, p. 53.
96. Imam Malik, *Muwatta,* Karachi, n.d., p. 570.
97. *Ibid.,* p. 570.
98. *Nail al-Autar,* Vol. 5 p. 141.
99. *Abu Daud, Tirmadhi, Nasai, Ibn-Majah.*
100. Chapra, M. Umer, Towards a *Just Monetary System,* Leicester, 1985, p. 57.
101. *Ibid.,* p. 217.
102. Naqvi, Syed Nawab Haider and Beg, Ahmed and Nazeer, *Principles of Islamic Economic Reform,* (PIDE) Islamabad, 1984, p. 52.
103. *Ibid.,* p. 30.
104. *Ibid.,* p. 23.
105. *Ibid.,* p. X.
106. *Ibid.,* p. 37.
107. *Ibid.,* p.41.
108. *Ibid.,* p.43.
109. *Ibid.,* p.37.
110. *Ibid.,* pp. 41-2
111. *Ibid.,* p. 48.
112. *Ibid.,* p. 11.
113. *Ibid.,* p. 37.
114. This and subsequent translations from Iqbal's *Javid Nama* are borrowed from *Pilgrimage of Eternity,* the present author's English translation of *Javid Nama.*
115. Keynes, *General Theory,* cit. op., pp. 374-5.
116. For detailed exposition, see *Man and Money,* Chapter III, Section 13.
117. *International Financial Statistics,* by I.M.F. Feb. 1979 read with Yearbook for 1981.
118. Percentages calculated from figures of deposits given in the above 1979 publication.
119. *International Financial Statistic Yearbook,* 1981.
120. *World Development Report,* 1987, p. 210.
121. Locke, John, *The Value of Money,* Ward, Lock and Co., London, *n.d.,* p. 610.
122. Samuelson, *Economics,* cit.op., p. 295.
123. *Ibid.,* p. 298.
124. *Ibid.,* p. 299.
125. *Ibid.,* p. 296.
126. Karunatilake H.N.S., *The Variable Reserve Ratio as an Instrument of Central Bank Policy,* Central Bank of Ceylon, 1963, p. 215.
127. Samuelson, *Economics,* cit.op., 299.
128. Tobin, James, "Financial Innovation and Deregulation in Perspective" in *Monetary Aid and Economic Studies,* Bank of Japan, Vol.3, No. 2, Sept., 1985, p. 215.
129. *Ibid.,* p. 24.
130. Samuelson, *Economics,* cit.op. p. 300.
131. Samuelson, Robert J. article in *Newsweek.* Feb. 3, 1986.
132. *The Quran,* 24:26. It means "provision honourable".
133. *International Financial Statistics Yearbook,* 1984, p. 555.
134. *Year Book of Labour Statistics,* 1981, p. 325.

135. *Pakistan Economic Survey*, 1984-85, p. 171.
136. *Ibid.*, 1985-86, p. 13.
137. Okun, Arthur M., *Political Economy of Prosperity* (Norton) New York, 1970, p. 137.
138. *Federal Budget in Brief*, 1987-88, p. 10.
139. *Ibid.*, p. 10.
140. The Railway Minister, Mr. Aslam Khan Khatak, is reported to have told the assembly on March 14, 1988 in answer to a question that in the year 1986-87, railway receipts were Rs 4.67 billion, its expenditure Rs 6.28 billion, and its loss Rs 1.61 billion *(Nawai Waqt,* March 15, 1988).
141. *Nawai Waqt,* March 15, 1988
142. In *Man and Money,* Chapter X , an identical exercise has been done in relation to budgetary deficit of U.S.A., and the conclusion reached is also identical.
143. Keynes, *General Theory,* cit. op., p. 376.
144. Karunatilake, H.N.S. *The Variable Reserve Ratio as an Instrument of Central Bank Policy, cit., op., p.215*
145. *Ibid.*, p. 221.
146. These are substitutes for debentures in which the return is a pre-agreed percentage of profits earned during the period of advances.
147. The theoretical argument behind this determining is omitted for the sake of brevity. Those who wish to go further into it may look up the last chapter of *Man and Money*.
148. All these tables are included in the last chapter of *Man and Money*.
149. 20% in this context means one fifth of the deficit that existed at the start of change over.
149.A, Newsweek, June 20, 1988, p. 40
150. Abu Daud, *Sunan,* English translation by Prof. Ahmad Hasan, Lahore, 1984, Vol. II p. 969.
151. Tariq, *Speeches and Statements of Iqbal,* cit. op., p. 8.
152. *Iqbal's Letters to Jinnah,* p. 17.
153. *Ibid.*, p. 18.
154. *Ibid.*, p. 18.
155. *Ibid.*, p. 19.
156. All figures are from *Annual Report* of State Bank of Pakistan for the year 1986-87, p. 136.
157. *Ibid.*, p. 149.
158. Quoted by Hawtrey, R.G., *A Century of Bank Rate,* Longmans, London, p. 31.
159. *Ibid.*, p. 31.
160. *Ibid.*, p. 31.
161. For the theoretical analysis of many of these examples and significant additional evidence see *Man and Money,* Chapter X Section 18.
162. Hawtrey, R.G., *A Century of Bank Rate,* cit. op., p. 246.
163. Keynes, *General Theory,*, cit. op., p. 339.
164. Hawtrey, R.G., *A Century of Bank Rate, cit. op., p. 139.*
165. Keynes, *A Treatise on Money,* Vol. II, p. 149.
166. Averages worked out from statistics provided in *International Financial Statistics Year-book* 1984, by I.M.F.
167. Smith, Hedrick, *The Russians,* Sphere Books, London, 1977 p. 248.
168. Monthly *"South"* London, May, 1988, p. 10.
169. Keynes, *General Theory of Employment, Interest, and Money*, pp. 213-4.
170. Cassel, G., *The Nature and Necessity of Interest*, Macmillan, London, 1903, p. 30.
171. Homer, Sidney, *A History of Interest Rates, cit., op.*, p. 153.
172. Tarshis, Lorie, in K.K. Kurihara's (Ed.) *Post-Keynesian Economics*, Allen and Unwin, London, 1955, p. 382.
173. Hawtrey, R.G., *Capital and Employment,* Longmans, London, 1938, p. 217.
174. Bronfenbrenner Martin, in Kurihara's (Ed) *Post-Keynesian Economics* cit. op., p. 56.
175. Detailed figures and appraisal are given in *Man and Money,* Chapter I, Section 6.
176. Keynes, *General Theory, cit., op.*, p. 221.

177. Kurihara, K.K., *Post-Keynesian Economics*, cit. op., p. 270.
178. *Elimination of Interest from the Economy*, State Bank of Pakistan Press, Karachi, 1980, p. 11.
179. Printed in 1980 by the State Bank of Pakistan Press, Karachi.
180. *The Elimination of Interest from the Economy*, p. 2.
181. *Ibid.*, pp. 8-9.
182. *Ibid.*, p. 11.
183. *Sood Ki Mutabadil Asas*, Institute of Islamic Culture, Lahore 1986.
184. *Report of the Council of Islamic Ideology*, 1980, Council of Islamic Ideology, Islamabad, p. 18.
185. Imam Malik, *Muwatta*, Karachi, n.d., p. 581.
186. *Ibid.*, p. 581.
187. *Ibid.*, p. 547.
188. *Ibid.*, p. 547.
189. Tabari, *Tafseer*, Bairut, Vol. IV, P. 59.
189–A Qutab, Sayyed, *Fi Zilal al-Quran*, Dar al-Sharuq, Beirut, 1973, Vol I, p. 324.
190. Khan, Mohammad Akram, *A Glossary of Islamic Economics*, 1987. p. 15
191. II-Corinthians, 3:6.
192. *al-Mughni*, Vol 3, p. 274.
193. *Musnad* Harith Bin Usama, quoted by Maulana Maudoodi in *Sood*, p. 236.
194. Gilani, Maulana Manazar Ahsan, *Islami Muashiat*, Hyderabad, 1947, p. 432.
195. Maudoodi, Maulana, *Sood*, p. 236.
196. The first article by the present writer on this subject appreared in "*Saqafat*", monthly Urdu journal of the Institute of Islamic Culture, Lahore, in October, 1960.
197. Khan, Mohammad Akram, *A Glossary of Islamic Economics*, 1987, p. 103.
198. *The Quran*, 55:60.
199. *The Quran*, 55:61.
200 Alhanafi, Ibn Nujaim, *al-Ashbahu WaL-Nazair*, p. 125, as quoted in *Islami Hikmate Maeeshat*, by Jama'te Islami, p. 151.
201. As quoted in *Islami Hikmate Maeeshat*, p. 153.
202. Matthew, 23:24.
203. *The Quran*, 2:42.

INDEX